The Royal Shakespeare Company

The Royal Shakespeare Company is one of the world's best known theatre ensembles, performing throughout the year in Stratford-upon-Avon, with regular residencies in London and Newcastle, and touring both in the UK and overseas.

We perform Shakespeare, modern classics and new plays. We also have a long tradition of adapting favourite young people's novels for our Christmas shows. Malorie Blackman's *Noughts & Crosses* has become a cult novel which young readers return to again and again. It has strong echoes of *Romeo and Juliet* and the RSC is proud to be working with such an influential writer.

Over the next few seasons we will be producing more new plays and inviting more living writers to become a major part of what we do. We are inviting writers into the Shakespeare rehearsal room and asking them to investigate the plays, to ask how the plays can be more engaging to young audiences, and also encouraging writers to imagine how Shakespeare would have approached his own plays, bringing the writers' viewpoint back into the rehearsal process.

Shakespeare is our in-house writer but we don't just produce his plays, we encourage contemporary writers to steal his ideas. We hope and believe that this re-connection of living writers with our house playwright will become one of the most mutually nourishing relationships in theatre. Shakespeare is a great teacher. His influence on writers cannot be underestimated. He knows how to marry the recognisable with the lyrical, and entertainment with high art. He knows how to marry the epic with the intimate. There is a vast array of skills and stagecraft which we are inviting contemporary dramatists to plunder – just so long as they roll their sleeves up and join the actors, directors, musicians and designers in wrestling Shakespeare's beauty and vigour onto our stages.

The Royal Shakespeare Company

Patron
Her Majesty the Queen

President
His Royal Highness
The Prince of Wales

Deputy President
Sir Geoffrey Cass

Artistic Director
Michael Boyd
Executive Director
Vikki Heywood

Board
Sir Christopher Bland (*Chairman*)
Professor Jonathan Bate FBA FRSL CBE
Neil W. Benson FCA OBE
Michael Boyd (*Artistic Director*)
Jane Drabble OBE
Mark Foster
Gilla Harris
Sara Harrity MBE
Vikki Heywood (*Executive Director*)
Laurence Isaacson CBE
Paul Morrell
Tim Pigott-Smith
Neil Rami
Lady Sainsbury of Turville (*Deputy Chairman*)

The RSC was established in 1961. It is incorporated under Royal
Charter and is a registered charity, number 212481.

SUPPORT THE RSC

As a registered charity the Royal Shakespeare Company relies on public support and generosity.

There are many ways you can help the RSC including joining Shakespeare's Circle, RSC Patrons, through Corporate support or by leaving a bequest.

RSC PATRONS AND SHAKESPEARE'S CIRCLE

By supporting the RSC through Shakespeare's Circle and RSC Patrons you can help us to create outstanding theatre and give as many people as possible a richer and fuller understanding of Shakespeare and theatre practice. In return you receive benefits including priority booking and invitations to exclusive supporters' events. Shakespeare's Circle Membership starts at £8.50 per month.

HELP SECURE OUR FUTURE

Legacy gifts ensure that the RSC can develop and flourish in the years to come, bringing the pleasure of theatre to future generations that you yourself have enjoyed.

CORPORATE PARTNERSHIPS

The RSC has a national and internationally recognised brand, whilst retaining its unique positioning as a Warwickshire based organisation. It tours more than any other UK based arts organisation and has annual residencies in London and Newcastle upon Tyne. As such it is uniquely placed to offer corporate partnership benefits across the globe.

The Company's experienced Corporate Development team can create bespoke packages around their extensive range of classical and new work productions, education programmes and online activity. These are designed to fulfill business objectives such as building client relationships, encouraging staff retention and accessing specific segments of the RSC's audience. A prestigious programme of corporate hospitality and membership packages are also available.

For more information, please telephone **01789 272283**

For detailed information about opportunities to support the work of the RSC, visit **www.rsc.org.uk/support**

This production of NOUGHTS & CROSSES was first performed
by the Royal Shakespeare Company at the Civic Hall,
Stratford-upon-Avon, on 29 November 2007.
The original cast was as follows:

Charles Abomeli	Jack/Mr Pingule/Executioner/ Man in the Café
Davinia Anderson	Dionne/Journalist/Juno
Doreene Blackstock	Kelani Adams/Governor/Lola
Daniel Bowers	Peter/Protestor
Michelle Butterly	Meggie
Louise Callaghan	Lynette/Leila
Christopher Daley	Colin/Morgan
Tyrone Huggins	Kamal/Mr Corsa
Tracy Ifeachor	Minerva
Richard Madden	Callum
Jo Martin	Jasmine
Phil McKee	Ryan
Jenny Ogilvie	Sarah Pike/Shania
Clarence Smith	Reporter/Policeman/Stanhope
Ony Uhiara	Sephy
Freddy White	Jude

All other parts played by members of the company

Directed by	**Dominic Cooke**
Designed by	**Kandis Cook**
Lighting designed by	**Wolfgang Göbbel**
Music by	**Gary Yershon**
Sound designed by	**Christopher Shutt**
Movement by	**Liz Ranken**
Fights by	**Terry King**
Assistant Director	**Rae Mcken**
Music Director	**Bruce O'Neil**
Dialect work by	**Penny Dyer**
Company voice work by	**Charmian Gradwell**
Casting by	**Sam Jones CDG**
Production Manager	**Pete Griffin**
Costume Supervisor	**Carrie Bayliss**
Company Stage Manager	**Pip Horobin**
Deputy Stage Manager	**Gabrielle Sanders**
Assistant Stage Manager	**Nicola Ireland**

for Alexi

NOUGHTS & CROSSES

Characters

NOUGHTS
Played by white actors

CALLUM MCGREGOR
MEGGIE MCGREGOR, *his mother*
RYAN MCGREGOR, *his father*
JUDE MCGREGOR, *his brother*
LYNETTE MCGREGOR, *his sister*
SHANIA, *a schoolchild*
COLIN, *a schoolchild*
LEILA, *a member of the Liberation Militia*
MORGAN, *a member of the Liberation Militia*
PETE, *a member of the Liberation Militia*
SARAH PIKE, *the Hadleys' Secretary*
FUNERAL GUESTS
SHOPPERS
BOMB-INJURY VICTIMS
RESCUE WORKERS
EXECUTION WITNESSES
PRISONERS

CROSSES
Played by black actors

SEPHY HADLEY
KAMAL HADLEY, *the Deputy Prime Minister, her father*
JASMINE HADLEY, *her mother*
MINERVA HADLEY, *her sister*
NEWS REPORTER
MR CORSA, *headmaster of Heathcroft High School*
JOANNE, *a schoolchild*
DIONNE, *a schoolchild*
LOLA, *a schoolchild*
STANHOPE

JUNO AYLETTE, *Kamal Hadley's PR*
KELANI ADAMS, *a barrister*
MR PINGULE, *a barrister*
PRISON GOVERNOR
JACK, *a prison guard*
CLERK OF COURT
SERGEANT COLLINS, *a policeman*
CONSTABLE JONES, *a policeman*
PRISON OFFICERS
STUDENTS
PROTESTORS
POLICEMEN
SHOPPERS
BOMB-INJURY VICTIMS
RESCUE WORKERS
KAMAL HADLEY'S ENTOURAGE
KAMAL HADLEY'S MINDER
EXECUTION WITNESSES
JOURNALISTS

Scenes should flow into one another with no gaps. No blackouts except where stated. There should be a minimum of props and clutter.

This text went to press before the end of rehearsals and so may differ slightly from the play as performed.

ACT ONE

Prologue

Sephy's Garden. A beautiful summer afternoon.

Enter JASMINE *and* MEGGIE *arm in arm, laughing.* CALLUM *and* SEPHY *are playing just offstage.*

JASMINE. Beautiful, it's beautiful.

MEGGIE. It was nothing, Mrs Hadley.

JASMINE. The balloons, the table, everything. You've excelled yourself, Meggie.

MEGGIE. Birthdays are important.

JASMINE. When you're eleven, they're everything. Callum's not thirteen for a while, is he?

MEGGIE. February.

JASMINE. The eleventh.

MEGGIE. You remembered.

JASMINE. I hope you're going to give him a party as lovely as this.

MEGGIE. Well, not quite on this scale.

Pause.

JASMINE. The other children will be here soon. Where has the birthday girl got to?

MEGGIE. In the rose garden. Playing with Callum.

JASMINE (*calling*). Persephone, nearly time to put on your party dress.

MEGGIE. Can I get you a cold drink?

JASMINE. It's quite all right, Meggie, I'll pour one for myself in a moment.

Pause.

Meggie, I know money's tight for you and Ryan.

MEGGIE. We're perfectly fine.

JASMINE. Well, I would very much like to pay for Callum's birthday party in February. As a gift.

MEGGIE. I couldn't possibly accept that, Mrs Hadley.

JASMINE. You're my friend, Meggie. You've been a fantastic friend to me, especially these last few months. And I like to look after my friends.

MEGGIE. That's very kind, Mrs Hadley, but even if I said yes, I know Ryan wouldn't be comfortable with it.

JASMINE. Well, let me speak to him nearer the time.

Enter SARAH.

SARAH. Excuse me, Mrs Hadley. I'm sorry to disturb you, but your husband has just arrived. He's in the study.

JASMINE. Kamal's here? Thank you, Sarah. (*To* MEGGIE.) His fourth trip home in as many months! Maybe he was able to get out of the state visit after all. Sephy will be over the moon.

JASMINE *goes into the house.*

MEGGIE. What's Mr Hadley doing here, Sarah? Is everything okay?

SARAH. Don't know.

MEGGIE. Is he in a good mood?

SARAH. Doesn't look too happy.

MEGGIE. What's wrong?

SARAH. No idea.

Pause.

I'd better get back to work.

MEGGIE. Would you like a cold drink? There's some ginger beer over there.

SARAH. No thanks. I don't want to get into trouble.

SARAH leaves.

MEGGIE. If there are any grass stains on those trousers, you'll be in big trouble, Callum.

KAMAL HADLEY *enters from the house behind* MEGGIE. JASMINE *follows him. She is nervous.*

KAMAL. Penny for your thoughts.

MEGGIE. Oh, Mr Hadley, you made me jump.

KAMAL. Something on your mind?

MEGGIE. I was just thinking about my son and your daughter.

KAMAL. What about them?

MEGGIE. Wouldn't it be nice if they could always stay as they are now? They're so wonderful at this age. Children, I mean – so . . . so –

KAMAL. Yes, indeed.

Pause.

I understand you had a lovely time yesterday evening.

MEGGIE. It was quite quiet really.

MEGGIE *looks towards* JASMINE.

KAMAL. So what did you do?

MEGGIE. Pardon?

KAMAL. Last night?

MEGGIE. We stayed at home and watched some telly.

KAMAL. A relaxing evening at home with the family. How nice.

MEGGIE. Yes.

KAMAL *stands up and goes to face his wife. He scrutinises her, then slaps her hard across the face.* KAMAL *goes back into the house.* MEGGIE *goes to* JASMINE.

Are you okay?

She reaches out to examine the side of JASMINE*'s face,* JASMINE *pushes her hand away.*

JASMINE. You stupid woman.

MEGGIE. I don't understand.

JASMINE. I told him I was with you last night. Couldn't you work it out?

MEGGIE. Oh, I'm so sorry, Mrs Hadley. I didn't . . .

JASMINE. No, you didn't. I believe it's time for Persephone to put on her party dress. Perhaps you could see to it.

MEGGIE. Yes, Mrs Hadley.

MEGGIE *turns towards the children.*

Sephy!

JASMINE *breaks down in tears, then walks back to the house.*

SEPHY *enters. It is three years later.*

Scene One

The Beach.

SEPHY (*to audience*). My family's private beach. This was my favourite place in the whole world. Kilometres of coastline that was all ours, with just a couple of signs saying 'Private Property', and some rickety old wooden fencing at each end, through which Callum and I had made a gap.

CALLUM *enters.*

(*To audience*.) This was the one place in the world where nobody else would find us. Since Callum's mum stopped working for my mum, we'd been meeting here every day. That was three years ago now. And we'd meet here every day for ever. No one could stop us.

SEPHY *and* CALLUM *sit together. The sound of waves.*

CALLUM. Can I kiss you?

SEPHY. Pardon?

CALLUM. Can I kiss you?

SEPHY. What on earth for?

CALLUM. Just to see what it's like.

SEPHY. Do you really want to?

CALLUM. Yeah I do.

SEPHY. Oh, all right then. But make it fast.

CALLUM *faces* SEPHY. *She tilts her head to the left. So does he. She tilts her head to the right. So does he.*

Do you want me to tilt my head to the left or the right?

CALLUM. Er, which side do girls normally tilt their heads when they're being kissed?

SEPHY. How should I know? Have I ever kissed a boy before?

CALLUM. Tilt your head to the left then.

SEPHY. My left or your left?

CALLUM. Er . . . your left.

She does so.

SEPHY. Hurry up, before I get a crick in my neck.

CALLUM *licks his lips and moves closer.*

Oh no you don't. Wipe your lips first.

CALLUM. Why?

SEPHY. You just licked them.

CALLUM. Oh. Okay.

CALLUM wipes his lips.

SEPHY. Hurry up.

CALLUM kisses SEPHY. After a moment, SEPHY withdraws.

Yuk! Callum! What did you do that for?

CALLUM. It wasn't that bad, was it?

SEPHY. I don't want your tongue on mine.

CALLUM. Why not?

SEPHY. 'Cause . . . our spit will mix up.

CALLUM. So? It's meant to.

SEPHY considers this.

SEPHY. Let's try it again.

They kiss again. After a while, SEPHY pulls away.

That's enough.

CALLUM. Sorry.

SEPHY. Why are you apologising? Didn't you like it?

CALLUM. It was . . . okay.

SEPHY. Have you ever kissed any girls besides me?

CALLUM. No.

SEPHY. Any Nought girls?

CALLUM. No.

SEPHY. Any Cross girls?

CALLUM. No means no.

SEPHY. So why do you want to kiss me?

CALLUM. We're friends, aren't we?

Pause.

SEPHY. What's the matter?

CALLUM. Nothing.

SEPHY. What're you thinking?

Pause.

CALLUM. Sephy, do you ever dream of just . . . escaping?
Hopping on the first boat or plane you come across and just
getting away from here.

SEPHY. This place isn't so bad, is it?

CALLUM. Depends on your point of view. You're on the inside.
With your dad's job and everything. You can't get much more
on the inside than the Deputy Prime Minister. Apart from the
Prime Minister.

SEPHY. If you do go away, will you take me with you?

CALLUM. We'd better get on with it.

He gets books out of his bag.

SEPHY. You've already passed the entrance exam. Why do we
still have to do this?

CALLUM. I don't want to give any of the teachers an excuse to
kick me out.

SEPHY. You haven't even started school yet and already you're
talking about being kicked out. You've got nothing to worry
about. You're in now. They accepted you.

CALLUM. Being in and being accepted are two different
things.

SEPHY. I've just had a thought. Maybe you'll be in my class.
Wouldn't that be great?

CALLUM. You think so?

SEPHY. Wouldn't you like to be in my class?

CALLUM. It's a bit humiliating for us Noughts to be stuck in the
baby class.

SEPHY. What d'you mean? I'm fourteen.

CALLUM. I'm nearly sixteen. How would you like to be in a class with kids two years younger than you?

SEPHY. The school explained why. You're at least a year behind and –

CALLUM. Noughts-only schools have no computers, hardly any books. My maths class last year had forty students. How many would you have at Heathcroft?

SEPHY. I dunno. Around fifteen.

CALLUM. Well, there you go then. Hardly our fault then, is it?

Pause.

Sorry. I didn't mean to bite your head off.

SEPHY. Are any of your friends from your old school going to join you at Heathcroft?

CALLUM. No. None of them got in. I wouldn't have either if you hadn't helped me.

Pause.

Come on, we'd better get back to work.

SEPHY. Okay. Maths or history?

CALLUM. Maths.

SEPHY. Yuk.

CALLUM. It's the universal language.

SEPHY. Pardon?

CALLUM. Look at how many different languages are spoken on our planet. The only thing that doesn't change, no matter what the language, is maths.

That's probably how we'll talk to aliens from other planets. We'll use maths.

SEPHY. Are you winding me up?

She gets her book out of her bag.

CALLUM. You should free your mind and think about other cultures and planets and, oh, I don't know, just think about the future.

SEPHY. I've got plenty of time to think about the future when I'm tons older and don't have much future left, thank you very much.

CALLUM. There's more to life than just us Noughts and you Crosses, you know.

SEPHY. Don't say that.

CALLUM. Don't say what?

SEPHY. *Us* Noughts and *you* Crosses. It makes it sound like . . . like I'm in one world and you're in another.

CALLUM. Maybe we are in different worlds.

SEPHY. We aren't if we don't want to be.

CALLUM. If only it was that simple.

SEPHY. It is.

CALLUM. Maybe from where you're sitting.

Pause.

SEPHY. How come I never go to your house any more? Aren't I welcome?

CALLUM. Course you are. But the beach is better.

SEPHY. Is it because of Lynette? 'Cause if it is, I really don't mind about your sister being . . .

CALLUM. Barking?

SEPHY. No, not 'barking', no.

CALLUM. Then what?

Pause.

SEPHY. Sorry.

CALLUM. Maybe it'd be better if we don't talk to each other when we're at school.

SEPHY. Why on earth not?

CALLUM. I don't want you to lose any of your friends because of me.

SEPHY. But that's just silly. They'll love you.

Silence.

What's wrong?

CALLUM. It's just. It doesn't matter. Give me a hug.

They go to hug.

JASMINE (*offstage*). PERSEPHONE! INSIDE! NOW!

SEPHY. Cripes! Mother.

CALLUM. You'd better go.

SEPHY. How did she find out I was here?

CALLUM. Just go.

SEPHY. But your lesson . . .

JASMINE (*offstage*). PERSEPHONE! WHAT ARE YOU DOING!

CALLUM. Hurry up.

SEPHY. See you tomorrow.

SEPHY grabs her things. She quickly kisses CALLUM on the lips and then runs off.

Scene Two

Callum's House.

CALLUM (*to audience*). Looking at our run-down hovel, I could feel the usual burning churning sensation begin to rise up inside me. My stomach tightened, my eyes began to narrow. Soon as I opened the front door, there was our living room with its fifth-hand threadbare nylon carpet and its seventh-hand cloth sofa. Why couldn't my family live in a house like Sephy's?

The MCGREGOR FAMILY *are now seated at the table.* CALLUM *moves around to each member as he introduces them.*

(*To audience.*) My family. Three years ago, Mum and Sephy's mother were really close. Mum was nanny to Sephy's sister, and then Sephy. One week, Mrs Hadley and Mum were like best friends, and the next week, Mum and I were no longer welcome anywhere near the Hadley house. No idea why. Dad isn't bothered about much – just keeps his head down. Jude, my seventeen-year-old brother, is a really irritating toad. Ever since I got into Heathcroft, he's become totally unbearable. Lynette, my sister; we've always been close. Closer than Jude and me. But something happened which changed Lynette. An accident. Now she doesn't go out, doesn't talk much, doesn't think much, as far as I can tell. She just is. 'Away with the fairies', as Grandma used to say. I can't get in and she doesn't come out. But her mind takes her to somewhere peaceful, I think. Sometimes I envy her.

The family are halfway through supper.

MEGGIE. Where've you been, Callum? I was worried sick.

CALLUM *sits*.

Well, I'm waiting. Where were you?

JUDE. He was with his Dagger friend.

MEGGIE. Don't use that word please, Jude.

CALLUM (*to audience*). Jude never called them Crosses. They were always Daggers.

MEGGIE. Well, were you with that girl again?

CALLUM. No, Mum, I went for a walk. That's all.

RYAN. Meggie, leave the lad alone.

MEGGIE. That had better be all.

MEGGIE serves CALLUM's food.

CALLUM. Hi, Lynny.

LYNETTE is in her own world.

You alright?

Pause.

MEGGIE. Where were you walking?

CALLUM. Oh, round and about.

MEGGIE. Hmmmm.

LYNETTE. What am I doing here?

Silence.

I shouldn't be here. I'm not one of you. I'm a Cross.

JUDE. What're you talking about? Look at your skin. You're just
   as white as the rest of us. Whiter.

LYNETTE. But my skin's a beautiful colour. So dark and rich and
   wonderful.

JUDE. I'm fed up with this. She's a ruddy nutter.

RYAN. Don't talk to your sister like that, please.

JUDE. And Callum's no better. Lord of the ruddy manor.

CALLUM. You don't know what you're talking about.

RYAN. We'd appreciate some peace and quiet at the dinner table.

JUDE. Look at you, peering down your nose at us just because
   you've come back from your precious Dagger girlfriend. You
   hate us and you hate yourself just because you weren't born
   one of them. I'm the only one of the three of us who knows
   what he is and is proud of it.

CALLUM. Shut up, you brainless . . .

*JUDE springs up, ready to hit CALLUM. CALLUM matches
him.*

JUDE. Come on then, if you think you're hard enough.

RYAN. I've had a very long day, Jude. Now stop it.

    CALLUM *slowly sits down*. JUDE *follows*.

LYNETTE. I can't be a Nought. I just can't.

MEGGIE. Listen, Lynette.

LYNETTE. I'm a Cross. Closer to God.

JUDE. Stupid cow.

RYAN. Jude!

LYNETTE. Don't you think I'm beautiful, Callum?

CALLUM. Yes I do, Lynette. Very.

    Pause.

RYAN. Ready for school tomorrow, Callum?

CALLUM. Ready as I'll ever be.

MEGGIE. I hope you're not making a mistake.

RYAN. He's not.

JUDE. He doesn't need to go to their schools. We don't have to mix with them.

CALLUM. What's wrong with mixing?

MEGGIE. It never works. We should be able to educate our own. Not wait for the Crosses to do it for us.

RYAN. You never used to believe that.

MEGGIE. Well I'm not as naïve as I used to be. Jasmine Hadley opened my eyes.

CALLUM (*to audience*). What would satisfy all the Noughts and Crosses who felt the same as Mum? Separate countries? Separate planets? How far away is far enough?

RYAN. Meggie, if our boy is going to get anywhere in this life, he has to learn to play the game. He has just got to be better at it than them. That's all.

MEGGIE. That's all!

RYAN. Don't you want something more for your son than we had?

MEGGIE. How can you ask me that?

CALLUM. I'm sure everything will be fine, Mum.

JUDE. You'll soon think you're too good for us.

RYAN. Of course he won't. You'll be on your best behaviour, won't you? You'll be representing all of us Noughts at the school.

CALLUM. Why do I have to represent all Noughts? Why can't I just represent myself?

RYAN. You must show them they're wrong about us. Show them we're just as good as they are.

MEGGIE. He doesn't need to go to their stuck-up school to show them that.

JUDE. He'll soon be as bad as they are.

RYAN. A son of mine at Heathcroft School. Imagine that!

Scene Three

School Gates.

SEPHY (*to audience*). First day of school. I groaned at the thought. At least today would be different from the start of every other new term. Three Noughts, including Callum, were starting at my school. I wanted to show him the playing fields and the swimming pool, the gym and music rooms, the dining hall and science labs. And I'd introduce him to all my friends. It was going to be wonderful. But as I approached the corner, shouting like an angry wave rolled towards me.

An angry Cross CROWD, *parents and students.*

CROWD. NO BLANKERS IN OUR SCHOOL! NO BLANKERS IN OUR SCHOOL! NO BLANKERS IN OUR SCHOOL!

MR CORSA. As the headmaster of this school it is my legal duty to ask you that you let the new students enter the school.

The CROWD *continues.*

CROWD. NO BLANKERS IN OUR SCHOOL! NO BLANKERS IN OUR SCHOOL!

SEPHY watches as CALLUM, COLIN *and* SHANIA, *all Noughts, try to push their way through the* CROWD *to get to the school entrance.* POLICE *try to push the* CROWD *into two separate groups.* MR CORSA *is in the other side of the* CROWD *looking on.* SHANIA *is hit by a stone.*

PROTESTOR 1. One of them is hurt.

PROTESTOR 2. A Blanker's hurt.

The CROWD *cheers. The struggle continues.* SEPHY *gets through.*

SEPHY. Mr Corsa, we have to help that girl. She's hurt!

He doesn't move.

(*Addressing the* CROWD.) Stop it! Just stop it!

CROWD. BLANKERS OUT! BLANKERS OUT!

SEPHY. STOP IT! YOU'RE ALL BEHAVING LIKE ANIMALS!

The CROWD *silences.*

WORSE THAN ANIMALS! LIKE BLANKERS!

As CALLUM *turns to the audience to speak, the* CROWD *melts away leaving* CALLUM *and* SEPHY *alone.*

CALLUM (*to audience*). She didn't say that. She couldn't have. Not Sephy . . . I'm not a Blanker. I may be a Nought but I'm worth more than nothing. I'm not a Blanker. A waste of time and space. A zero. A nothing.

Scene Four

The Beach.

SEPHY. Callum, don't look at me like that.

Pause.

What would you like me to say?

Pause.

I said I'm sorry.

CALLUM. I know.

SEPHY. It's just a word.

CALLUM. Just a word . . .

SEPHY. Sticks and stones, Callum. It's one word, that's all.

CALLUM. If you'd slapped me or kicked me or punched me or
even stabbed me it would've stopped hurting sooner or later.
But I'll never forget what you called me, Sephy. Never. Not if
I live to be five hundred.

SEPHY. I didn't mean it. I didn't mean you. I was trying to help.

CALLUM. Sephy . . .

SEPHY. Please, I'm so sorry.

CALLUM. Maybe we shouldn't see so much of each other any
more.

SEPHY. Callum, no. I said I was sorry.

Pause.

CALLUM. Promise me something.

SEPHY. Anything.

CALLUM. Promise me that you'll never ever use that word
again.

SEPHY. I promise.

(*To audience.*) I'd never fully realised just how powerful words could be. Whoever came up with that 'sticks and stones may break my bones' rubbish was talking out of their armpit. Why did I say that word? It was as if I was outside myself. More and more I was beginning to feel like a spectator in my own life. I had to make a choice. I had to decide what kind of friend Callum was going to be to me.

Scene Five

Callum's House. At the dinner table.

RYAN. Are you okay, son? I went down to Heathcroft as soon as I heard what was going on, but the police wouldn't let me in.

CALLUM. Why not?

RYAN. I had 'no official business on the premises' – unquote.

JUDE. Those rotten, stinking –

MEGGIE. Jude, not at the dinner table, please.

RYAN. So how was school? How were your lessons, son?

CALLUM. It was fine, Dad. (*To audience.*) Except that the teachers totally ignored us, and the Crosses used any excuse to bump into us and knock our books on the floor, and even the dinner ladies made sure they served everyone else in the queue before us. (*To* RYAN.) It was fine.

RYAN. You're in there now, Callum. Don't let any Dagger swine drive you out – you understand?

MEGGIE. Excuse me. But when I say I don't want that word used at the dinner table, that applies to everyone. Including you, Ryan.

RYAN. Sorry, love.

CALLUM (*to* LYNETTE). Have a good day, Lynny?

Pause.

JUDE. You were on the telly. So was your little friend. The whole world heard what she said.

CALLUM. She didn't mean it like that.

JUDE. She didn't mean it? That's what she told you, was it? How can you not mean to say something like that?

MEGGIE. I see Miss Sephy is turning out to be just like her mother.

RYAN. You're better off without that job.

MEGGIE. You don't have to tell me twice. I admit I miss the money but I wouldn't go back for all the stars in space. Anyone who can put up with that stuck-up cow Mrs Hadley is a saint, as far as I'm concerned.

CALLUM. You were friends once.

MEGGIE. Friends? We were never friends. She patronised me and I put up with it 'cause I needed a job – that's all.

CALLUM (*to audience*). That wasn't how I remembered it.

RYAN *clicks his remote.*

RYAN. Shush, everyone. The news is on.

The NEWS REPORTER, *a Cross, enters the* MCGREGORS' *kitchen, perhaps sitting at the table. When reading the news, the* REPORTER *speaks directly to the other characters on stage. This convention is used whenever the TV is being watched. There is no TV set or video screen on stage.*

REPORTER (*to the family*). Today Kamal Hadley, Home Office Minister, declared that there would be no hiding place, no safe haven, for those Noughts misguided enough to join the Liberation Militia.

(*Addressing someone offstage.*) Is it true, Mr Hadley, that your government's decision to allow selected Noughts in our schools was a direct result of pressure from the Liberation Militia?

KAMAL *enters the kitchen.*

KAMAL. Not at all. This government does not allow itself to be manipulated by illegal terrorist groups. We acted on a Pangean Economic Community directive that the government had been on the verge of implementing anyway. Our decision to allow the crème de la crème of Nought youth to join our educational institutions makes sound social and economic sense.

CALLUM (*to audience*). Pompous twit!

KAMAL. The Liberation Militia are misguided terrorists and we will leave no stone unturned in our efforts to bring them to justice.

JUDE. Long live the Liberation Militia!

RYAN. Too right, son.

MEGGIE. Shhh.

JUDE *and* RYAN *look at each other.*

REPORTER. There have been unconfirmed reports that the car bomb found outside the International Trade Centre last month was the work of the Liberation Militia. What attempts are being made to find those responsible?

KAMAL. I can tell you that our highest priority is to find those responsible and bring them to justice. Political terrorism which results in the death or serious injury of even one Cross always has been and always will be a capital crime. Those found guilty will suffer the death sentence . . .

SEPHY *enters with her own remote which she clicks. The* REPORTER *and* KAMAL *leave the stage.*

SEPHY (*to audience*). Politics, politics, politics. I've grown up with it rammed down my throat. I'm not interested in being caught up with it in any manner, shape or form, whether Dad is on the telly or not.

Scene Six

The School Dining Hall. The school bell rings.

CALLUM (*to audience*). I lined up in the food queue. I collected my chicken and mushroom pie with boiled-to-death trimmings, my jam tart with custard and my carton of milk and, taking a deep breath, I headed for the table where the other Noughts were sitting.

SEPHY approaches the Noughts' table. SHANIA wears a large brown plaster on her face.

SEPHY. Do you mind if I join you?

She sits at the table.

CALLUM. What do you think you're doing?

SEPHY. Sitting down.

CALLUM. Go away, Sephy.

SEPHY. Why should I? I want to sit here.

CALLUM moves to another seat. SEPHY smiles at the other Noughts who have been staring at her. They instantly look away. She offers SHANIA her hand.

Hi. I'm Sephy Hadley. Welcome to Heathcroft.

SHANIA wipes her hand clean on her clothes. She then takes SEPHY's hand and shakes it slowly.

SHANIA. I'm Shania.

SEPHY. That's a pretty name. What does it mean?

SHANIA. It doesn't mean anything.

SEPHY. My mother told me my name means 'serene night'. But Callum will tell you, I'm anything but serene.

SHANIA smiles tentatively.

How's your cut?

SHANIA. It's okay. It'll take more than a stone to dent my head.

SEPHY. The plaster's a bit noticeable.

SHANIA. They don't sell pink plasters. Only dark brown ones.

SEPHY. Oh. I suppose they do.

MR CORSA approaches.

MR CORSA. Sephy, just what do you think you're doing?

SEPHY. Pardon?

MR CORSA. What're you doing?

SEPHY. I'm eating my lunch.

MR CORSA. Don't be facetious.

SEPHY. I'm not. I'm eating my lunch.

MR CORSA. Get back to your own table – at once.

Everyone in the dining hall watches, engrossed.

SEPHY. But I want to sit here.

MR CORSA. Get back to your own table – NOW!

SEPHY. I'm sitting with my friend Callum.

MR CORSA grabs SEPHY's arm and pulls her out of the chair.

MR CORSA. Persephone Hadley, you will come with me.

As SEPHY is dragged away she looks at CALLUM. He looks away.

SHANIA. Serves her right. Coming over to our table and acting the big 'I am'.

CALLUM. She didn't. It wasn't like that.

SHANIA. Of course it was. She wanted to lord it over us. A little kid like that, sitting at our table.

CALLUM. What're you talking about?

SHANIA. Just because her dad's in the government, that Sephy
    Hadley thought she'd play Lady Magnanimous and sit with us.
    I bet she'll go and scrub her hand now I shook it.

The dining hall melts away, leaving CALLUM.

CALLUM (*to audience*). I walked out of the food hall and out of
    the building and out of the school, my steps growing ever faster
    and more frantic – until by the time I was out of the school I
    was running. Running until my back ached and my feet hurt
    and my heart was ready to burst, and still I kept running. I ran
    all the way out of the town and down to the beach.

CALLUM *collapses on the sand and punches his bag over
and over.*

SEPHY! SEPHY! SEPHY!

SEPHY *approaches. She stares at* CALLUM, *full of anger.*

SEPHY. Turning your back on me like that. Some best friend.

CALLUM. Alright, alright.

Pause.

SEPHY. You're a snob, Callum. And I never realised it until now.
    I thought you were better than that. Above all that nonsense.
    But you're just like all the others. 'Crosses and Noughts
    shouldn't be friends. Crosses and Noughts shouldn't even live
    on the same planet together.'

CALLUM. That's rubbish. I don't believe any of that, you know I
    don't.

SEPHY. Well, if you're not a snob, you're a hypocrite, which is
    even worse. I'm okay to talk to as long as no one can see us.
    As long as no one knows.

CALLUM. Don't talk to me like that.

SEPHY. Which one is it, Callum? Are you a snob or a hypocrite?

CALLUM. Get lost, Sephy.

SEPHY. With pleasure.

SEPHY *goes to leave.*

CALLUM. I'm sorry.

SEPHY. I thought that was my job in this friendship. Saying sorry. Sorry for being at a good school. Sorry for saying the wrong thing. Sorry for sitting at your table. I'm sick of feeling guilty all the time. It's not my fault that things are the way they are.

CALLUM. I know.

SEPHY. Then stop blaming me. And if you can't, then leave me alone.

She exits.

CALLUM (*to audience*). Why had my life suddenly become so complicated? For the last year all I could ever think about was going to school. Sephy's school. I was so busy concentrating on getting into Heathcroft that I didn't give any thought to what it'd be like when I actually got there.

Scene Seven

Girl's Toilets.

SEPHY (*to audience*). There is a proverb which says, 'Be careful what you wish for, because you might just end up getting it!' I never really knew what that meant until now. All those months helping Callum with his work so he'd pass the Heathcroft entrance exam and we could go to the same school together, be in the same class together even. And now it had all come true. And it was horrible. Everything was going wrong. Well . . . I couldn't hide in a toilet cubicle for ever. And who was I hiding from anyway? Well, all those people who'd been pointing and whispering as I walked past them in the school corridor for starters – but mainly from Callum. I was afraid to face him. If I didn't see him, I could pretend nothing between us had changed.

The school bell rings.

(*To audience.*) Okay! Here goes. I drew back the bolt and opened the cubicle door.

Three Cross girls, LOLA, JOANNE *and* DIONNE, *confront* SEPHY.

LOLA. We want to have a word with you.

SEPHY. And it has to be in here, does it, Lola?

JOANNE *shoves* SEPHY.

JOANNE. About what you did yesterday.

SEPHY. What's it to you?

LOLA *slaps* SEPHY.

LOLA. I don't care if your dad's God Almighty Himself. Stick to your own kind. If you sit with the Blankers again, everyone in this school will treat you like one of them.

JOANNE. You need to wake up and check which side you're on.

DIONNE. What d'you want to be around them for anyway? They smell funny and they eat weird food and everyone knows that none of them are exactly close friends with soap and water.

The three GIRLS *laugh.*

SEPHY. What a load of rubbish. Callum has a wash every day and he doesn't smell. None of them do.

LOLA, JOANNE *and* DIONNE *look at each other.* LOLA *pushes* SEPHY *down on the toilet seat.*

SEPHY *tries to stand.* LOLA *pushes her down again.*

LOLA. We're only going to say this once. Choose your friends very carefully. If you don't stay away from those Blankers, you'll find you don't have a single friend left in this school.

SEPHY. I bet none of you has even spoken to a Nought before.

JOANNE. Of course we have. When they serve us in shops and restaurants . . .

DIONNE. In burger bars!

They laugh.

JOANNE. Besides, we don't need to speak to them. We see them
on the news practically every other day. Everyone knows
they're all muggers and they hang around in gangs and knife
people and listen to crap music.

LOLA. Look at the facts. It's on the news. The news doesn't lie.

SEPHY. The news lies all the time. They tell us what they think
we want to hear. The majority of Noughts are decent, hard-
working people.

JOANNE. Who told you that? Your dad?

LOLA. I bet it was one of her Blanker friends. Blank by name
and blank by nature.

SEPHY. What are you talking about?

LOLA. Blank, white faces with not a hint of colour in them.
Blank minds which can't hold a single original thought. Blank,
blank, blank.

SEPHY. You ought to sell that horse manure worldwide. You'd
make a fortune. Noughts are people, just like us. You're the
ones who are stupid and ignorant and . . .

LOLA *slaps* SEPHY. SEPHY *punches* LOLA *in the stomach.*
She continues hitting LOLA. LOLA *and* JOANNE *grab one of*
SEPHY*'s arms.*

DIONNE. Blanker-lover. You've had this coming for a long time.

DIONNE *beats up* SEPHY.

Scene Eight

Outside Sephy's House.

CALLUM (*to audience*). When Shania told me the news about Sephy, my feet scarcely touched the ground. I didn't stop until I was standing in front of the Hadleys' iron gates.

CALLUM, *on one side of the stage, presses the entryphone for a long time.* SARAH *appears. As with the TV's, there are no real phones.*

SARAH. Yes?

CALLUM. Sephy?

SARAH. This is Mrs Hadley's secretary.

CALLUM. Sarah, it's Callum McGregor. I want to see Sephy – please.

SARAH. I'm afraid the doctor says she's not to be disturbed.

The sound of the receiver being replaced. SARAH *exits.* CALLUM *puts his finger on the buzzer and holds it there.* SARAH *re-enters.*

Yes?

He stops buzzing.

CALLUM. I want to see Sephy. Is she all right?

SARAH. She's badly bruised and very upset. The doctor has advised that she be kept at home for the rest of the week.

CALLUM. What happened? Why?

JASMINE (*offstage*). Who is it, Sarah?

SARAH. It's all under control, Mrs Hadley.

JASMINE (*offstage*). Is it that McGregor boy?

SARAH. Yes, Mrs Hadley.

Enter JASMINE. *She takes the receiver from* SARAH.

JASMINE. This is Persephone's mother, can I help you?

CALLUM. I'd like to see Sephy, please.

JASMINE. I believe my daughter was attacked by three girls for sitting at your lunch table yesterday. As I understand it, you turned your back on her and told her to go away. Is that right?

CALLUM. I was trying to protect her. I didn't want her to get bullied for being my friend.

JASMINE. Hmmm.

JASMINE *hands the receiver back to* SARAH.

Sarah, make sure this boy doesn't set foot in here again.

CALLUM. Please let me see Sephy.

SARAH. You're going to have to go now.

CALLUM. Please . . .

SARAH. I'm sorry.

SARAH *exits*.

Scene Nine

Sephy's Bedroom.

SEPHY (*to audience*). There was absolutely nothing on the telly. What a choice. Silly cartoons, a brainless quiz game, the news or a war film. With a sigh I plumped for the news. I looked at the screen without really watching it. The newsreader was finishing the story of a stockbroker who'd been sent to prison for fraud. He was now talking about three Nought robbers who'd smashed in the front of an exclusive jewellery store and made off on motorbikes with gems and jewellery and watches worth close to a million. Why was it that when Noughts committed criminal acts, the fact that they were Noughts was always pointed out? The stockbroker was a Cross. The newsreader didn't even mention it.

She flicks off the TV.

(*To audience*.) I closed my eyes. I tried to find something to focus on besides the bruises over my body. Callum . . . Even thinking about him wasn't bringing me the comfort it usually did. My best friend had turned his back on me. Not a word since Lola and the others laid into me. I knew I was feeling well and truly sorry for myself, but I couldn't help it. Ruddy Noughts. This was all their fault. If it hadn't been for them . . . And as for Lola and her stooges, I was going to get them, if it was the very last thing I did. I was going to get them – and good. I opened my eyes and stared out into nothing but hate.

Scene Ten

Callum's House. Evening.

There is a mirror onstage. LYNETTE *and* JUDE *are squaring up to each other.*

LYNETTE. You're a git, Jude, and a vulgar git at that!

JUDE. At least I'm not living a lie.

LYNETTE. And what's that supposed to mean?

JUDE. You're white. Face it.

CALLUM. Leave her alone, Jude, you bully.

JUDE *hits* LYNETTE. *She hits him back. They start fighting and* RYAN *comes between them.*

JUDE. Look at you! You think you're too damn good to breathe the same air as us. Well, I've got news for you. When the Daggers look at you, they see someone who's just as white as me.

LYNETTE. I'm not like you. I'm different.

JUDE *pushes past* RYAN.

RYAN. Stop it, Jude.

JUDE *grabs* LYNETTE *and takes her to the mirror. He forces her to look at their reflection.*

JUDE. See! You're the same as me. As white as me. I'm sick and tired of you looking down your nose at me. If you hate what you are, do something about it. Just die or something! And if there is a God, you'll come back as one of those ruddy Daggers you love so much, and then I can stop feeling guilty about hating you.

LYNETTE *falls to the floor.*

CALLUM. Do something, Dad.

RYAN. Jude, that's enough. More than enough.

JUDE. It's time she heard the truth from someone. Who else is going to say it?

CALLUM. You're always so sure you're right, aren't you? You make me sick. Lynette isn't the only one here who can't stand you.

JUDE. She's a waste of space.

RYAN (*to* JUDE). What the hell is wrong with you? She's your sister, for goodness' sake.

JUDE. Oh, get lost, Dad.

RYAN *spins* JUDE *around and slaps his face.*

RYAN. Don't you ever, ever talk to me like that. I'm too old and have had to contend with too much crap in my life to put up with disrespect in my own house. You have no idea what your sister's been through, so how dare you judge her?

JUDE. Yeah yeah yeah, we all know, she had an accident. Poor little Lynny. That was three years ago. Isn't it time she got over it?

RYAN. You don't know the first thing about what your sister's been through.

JUDE. She's just a spoiled little princess.

RYAN. I'd like to see you cope with what happened to her. You wouldn't have lasted five minutes.

CALLUM. It wasn't an accident, was it?

Pause.

RYAN. Lynny and her boyfriend were attacked. By our own. Three or four Nought men beat Lynette's lad nearly to death. And she was so badly hurt she had to spend two weeks in hospital.

CALLUM. I knew it. I knew there was something you weren't telling us.

JUDE. Why didn't she want us to know?

RYAN. Because her boyfriend was a Cross.

JUDE. I might have guessed.

RYAN. She was so ashamed she begged us not to tell you.

JUDE. Maybe that will teach her to stick to her own kind.

RYAN. Your sister was put into intensive care by those animals. They left her for dead. Is it any wonder that she can't bear to think of herself as one of us any more? Now leave her alone. Or you'll have me to answer to. D'you hear me? Jude, do you hear me?

Pause.

JUDE. Yes, Dad.

LYNETTE. Where's Jed, Daddy?

RYAN. Honey, Jed went away a long, long time ago. Let me get you up.

LYNETTE. Where am I?

RYAN. At home. You're safe now. I'm here.

CALLUM. We'll look after you, Lynny.

LYNETTE. Where's Jed?

RYAN. Listen, sweetheart, Jed and his family moved away a long time ago. He's gone.

LYNETTE. Not a long time ago. Yesterday. Last week.

RYAN. It was years ago.

LYNETTE. It's my eighteenth birthday next week.

RYAN. No, love, you're twenty. Twenty last April. Come on, let's get up.

LYNETTE. I thought I was seventeen. Eighteen. I don't know what I thought.

RYAN. Lynette, please –

JUDE reaches out his hand to LYNETTE.

JUDE. I'm sorry, Lynny.

She takes JUDE's hand and puts it next to hers. She looks at them closely.

LYNETTE. Your hands are the same as mine. The same as theirs.

LYNETTE goes to exit.

CALLUM. I'll come with you.

LYNETTE. No, I'll be all right.

LYNETTE exits. JUDE and RYAN look at each other.

CALLUM (*to audience*). I caught sight of the three of us in the mirror. My face was the reflection of Dad and Jude. My expression was theirs. My thoughts and feelings and hates and fears were all theirs, just as theirs were mine, and though I like to think I'm quick and on the ball, I hadn't even realised. Until now.

Scene Eleven

The Classroom. Maths lesson.

SEPHY (*to audience*). Jeez! Time crawled like it was dragging a blue whale behind it. That sounded like something Callum would say – something Callum would've said – when he used to talk to me. When he used to be my friend. The teacher was blathering on about simultaneous equations like they were the best thing since computers were invented. And every word was flying zip-zap straight over my head. When was the bell going to sound? Come on . . . come on . . .

The school bell rings.

(*To audience.*) At last!

SEPHY *gathers her books up and makes to leave.*

CALLUM. Sephy, wait.

SEPHY *sits.*

How are you? Are you okay now?

SEPHY. Yes, thank you.

CALLUM. I'm glad.

SEPHY. Are you? You could have fooled me.

CALLUM. What does that mean?

Other STUDENTS *are listening.*

SEPHY. Don't pretend you were worried about me. You didn't come and see me once. You didn't even send me a 'Get Well Soon' card.

CALLUM. I came to see you every day. Every single day. Your mum gave orders that I wasn't to be let in. I stood outside your gates every afternoon after school. Ask your mum . . . no, ask Sarah Pike if you don't believe me.

Pause.

Wild horses couldn't have kept me away.

SEPHY. I have to go now.

CALLUM. Look, meet me in our special place after dinner tonight. We can't talk here.

She turns to walk away.

If you're not there, I'll understand.

SEPHY. Goodbye, Callum.

Scene Twelve

Callum's Bedroom.

CALLUM (*to audience*). Since Lynny and Jude's fight, neither of them had spoken to each other. Not a word. That evening, as I was finishing my homework, there was a knock at my bedroom door . . .

LYNETTE. It's me. Can I come in?

CALLUM. Course.

> LYNETTE *comes in.*

> You okay?

LYNETTE. No. You?

CALLUM. I'll survive.

LYNETTE. How's school?

CALLUM. Well, I'm learning a lot.

LYNETTE. Tough going?

CALLUM. Nightmare.

LYNETTE. Reckon you'll stick with it?

CALLUM. I'm in now. I'm not about to let them push me out.

LYNETTE. How do you do it, Callum?

CALLUM. Do what?

LYNETTE. Keep going.

> *Pause.*

CALLUM. I suppose because I know what I want.

LYNETTE. Which is?

> *Pause.*

CALLUM. To be someone. To make a difference, I guess.

LYNETTE. Which means more to you? Being someone or making a difference?

CALLUM *laughs*.

What's so funny?

CALLUM. Nothing. It's just that you and me talking like this, it reminds me of the old days.

LYNETTE. You haven't answered my question, and don't try to wriggle out of it! Which means more – being someone or making a difference?

CALLUM. I don't know. Being someone I guess. Having a large house and money in the bank and not needing to work and being respected wherever I go. When I'm educated and I've got my own business there won't be a single person in the world who'll be able to look down on me – Nought or Cross.

LYNETTE. Being someone, eh? I would've put money on you choosing the other one!

CALLUM. What's the point in making a difference if you've got nothing to show for it personally, if there's not even any money in it?

Pause.

Are you disappointed in me?

LYNETTE. You've always been so focused. You've always known exactly where you wanted to end up. I hope it works out for you.

Pause.

You know what I miss? I miss being bonkers!

CALLUM. Don't say that.

LYNETTE. I do. I know I was living in a fantasy world before, but at least I was somewhere. Now I'm nowhere.

CALLUM. That's not true.

LYNETTE. Isn't it?

Pause.

CALLUM. Lynny, d'you remember my seventh birthday? You took me to see my first film at the cinema. There was just you and me in the whole place and you got annoyed because I wouldn't take my eyes off the screen. Not for a second.

LYNETTE. I told you you were allowed to blink. D'you remember? That the screen wasn't going to disappear.

Pause.

CALLUM. Lynny, you are all right, aren't you?

LYNETTE. I don't know.

CALLUM. Things will get better.

LYNETTE. I want to believe that. I really do.

CALLUM. I'm at Heathcroft High, aren't I? A few years ago that would have been impossible. Unthinkable.

LYNETTE. But none of their universities will take you.

CALLUM. You don't know that. By the time I'm ready to leave school they might.

LYNETTE. And then what?

CALLUM. I'll get a good job. And I'll be on my way up.

LYNETTE. Doing what?

CALLUM. You sound just like Jude.

LYNETTE *goes to leave.*

Sorry. That was below the belt.

She stops.

It's not too late for you to go to college.

LYNETTE. How would we pay for that? Anyway, I'm not like you. I don't have what it takes.

CALLUM. Of course you do. You've never given yourself the chance.

LYNETTE. Just remember, when you're floating up and up in your bubble, that bubbles burst. The higher you climb, the further you have to fall.

She exits.

Scene Thirteen

The Beach.

CALLUM. Persephone, you have to believe me. I did come to visit you, I swear.

Pause.

SEPHY. I believe you.

CALLUM. You spoke to Sarah.

SEPHY. Didn't have to.

CALLUM. I don't understand.

SEPHY. I just believe you. Besides, it sounds like the sort of thing my mother would do.

Pause.

It'll be winter soon. It'll be harder for me to come and meet you here. Mother won't allow it.

CALLUM. Who beat you up?

SEPHY. What does it matter?

CALLUM. You don't want them to get away with it, do you?

SEPHY. There's not a lot I can do about it now. I was going to tell Corsa and get them expelled or put drawing pins in their shoes or whatever, but they're not worth it. I don't want to waste any more energy on them. It happened and now it's over, and I just want to forget about it.

CALLUM. I was just curious. Besides, what could I do? I'm just a lowly Nought. Not on their level. Or yours.

SEPHY. Stop it.

CALLUM. Stop what?

SEPHY. Callum, it's me. Sephy. I'm not your enemy.

CALLUM. I never said . . .

SEPHY takes CALLUM's face in her hands.

SEPHY. Look at me, Callum.

He is tense, resisting. Then he starts to relax.

I'm your friend and I always will be.

CALLUM. Sorry.

They hug. SEPHY lets go of him.

Scene Fourteen

Callum's House.

CALLUM (*to audience*). When I got home, Lynette was missing.

MEGGIE. Jude and Lynette, fighting? Ryan, I can't believe you stood by and let it happen. I go to visit my sister for one evening and the whole family falls apart. Why didn't you tell me what had happened? You are the most ineffectual, useless man it's ever been my misfortune to come across.

JUDE. It's not Dad's fault, Mum.

MEGGIE. And you can shut right up. I'm sick to the back teeth of this belief you have, that you and your opinions are always right. You've been picking on your sister and goading her for months now.

JUDE. Well, you've been picking on me, so that makes us about even.

MEGGIE. I've been picking on you – as you call it – because you're not doing anything with your life. You could work with your dad in the lumberyard or do an apprenticeship with Old Man Tony but –

JUDE. Old Man Tony is always bombed off his trolley! Light a match in front of his mouth and the whole street would go up in flames. And I don't want to get stuck in his ruddy bakery.

MEGGIE. It's an honest job.

JUDE. I don't want an honest job.

MEGGIE. You don't know what you want.

JUDE. Yes, I do. I want to go back to school.

CALLUM (*to audience*). Since when did Jude want to go back to school?

MEGGIE. Jude, we've been through this before. We didn't have the money to keep you in school. I lost my job, remember? Aren't you going to stand up for me, Ryan? Will you always be such an ineffectual, useless –

JUDE. But you found the money for Callum to go.

The doorbell rings.

RYAN goes offstage to answer it.

COLLINS (*offstage*). Mr McGregor?

RYAN (*offstage*). Yes?

COLLINS (*offstage*). May we come in?

RYAN (*offstage*). Please.

Two Cross policemen enter with RYAN. LYNETTE walks behind them.

COLLINS. I'm Sergeant Collins and this is Constable Jones.

RYAN. Officers?

COLLINS. You have a daughter called Lynette?

MEGGIE. What's happened?

COLLINS. I'm very sorry, sir, ma'am. I'm afraid I've got some bad news.

They all freeze behind CALLUM. LYNETTE *watches.*

CALLUM (*to audience*). When the police told us the news, Lynette entered my head and filled my thoughts and spun around me and danced through me until it felt like she was swallowing me up. Mum let out a howl like a wounded animal and sank to her knees. Jude took a step forward and then stopped. The two police officers looked away. The seconds ticked past. Dad hugged Mum, rocking her. Mum didn't speak and she didn't cry. She didn't make a sound.

The family leave the room. LYNETTE *stays.*

(*To audience.*) For the first time in my life, I hated my sister. Hated her guts. She'd given in. She'd given up on life and left me to live it for the both of us. From that moment, I swore that nothing would ever make me do the same as her. Nothing.

Scene Fifteen

Callum's House. Lynette's wake.

SEPHY (*to audience*). It'd only been three years since Callum's mum had worked for mine. Three short years. But walking into his house was like walking into a room full of strangers.

The room is filled entirely with NOUGHT GUESTS, *huddled in groups.* JUDE *is tipsy.* MEGGIE *and* RYAN *are close together.* SEPHY *approaches* MEGGIE *and* RYAN. *The room goes quiet.*

Mr and Mrs McGregor, I just wanted to tell you how sorry I am about Lynette. I hope I'm not intruding or anything.

MEGGIE. You're not intruding, Persephone. Thank you for coming. Can I get you a drink?

SEPHY *looks around at the hostile faces staring at her.*

SEPHY. No, I don't think I should stay.

MEGGIE. Nonsense. You've come this far, you can't leave without a drink. Can she, Ryan?

Pause.

Ryan?

Pause.

SEPHY. I'll go.

CALLUM. Sephy –

JUDE. Who told you to come here in the first place? You and your false sympathy aren't wanted.

MEGGIE. Jude, that's enough.

JUDE. If she cares so much, where was she for the last three years when Lynette was out of her head and we didn't have two beans to rub together to get her the help she needed? Where was this Dagger when you got fired, Mum, and I had to drop out of school?

JUDE gives SEPHY a shove. Some GUESTS gasp.

And then you have the gall to come over here –

SEPHY. Mrs McGregor, Mr McGregor –

RYAN. Just go, Miss Hadley.

SEPHY. But I haven't done anything –

RYAN. That's right, you haven't. You come in here, with your designer dress which cost more than I make in a year, and we're supposed to be grateful. Is that how it works?

SEPHY. No –

JUDE. Just go away. Go on, get out, before I do something I regret.

CALLUM guides SEPHY's arm.

CALLUM. Sephy, I'll –

RYAN. Let her go. Noughts and Crosses don't mix, son.

SEPHY *rushes out. The* GUESTS *resume talking.*

MEGGIE (*to* JUDE). You had no right to do that.

RYAN. Oh yes he did. She wasn't wanted here. Jude told her the truth.

JUDE. Good on you, Dad.

MEGGIE. The girl wasn't doing any harm, Ryan. She only came here out of sympathy.

RYAN. Out of guilt, more like.

MEGGIE. She was paying her respects.

RYAN. She and her kind can go to hell. I don't want those Daggers anywhere near me.

MEGGIE. Ryan!

RYAN. I've had enough, Meggie. I've had enough. My ineffectual days are over.

CALLUM (*to audience*). I thought Dad's motto was 'Live and let live'. When did that change? When Lynny died? Or maybe it was there all the time and I'd just chosen not to see it.

Scene Sixteen

The Beach.

CALLUM *and* SEPHY *sit as before.*

SEPHY. I didn't mean any harm, Callum.

CALLUM. Well, *I* know that but . . .

SEPHY. But it wasn't the best idea I've ever had in my life.

CALLUM. You've had better.

SEPHY. I can't seem to do anything right at the moment.

Beat.

I am sorry about your sister, Callum. I just wanted to show how much . . . I thought sending a card would be a bit . . .

CALLUM. Impersonal?

SEPHY. Exactly. It was just a spur-of-the-moment thing to walk over to your house. I thought it might be a comfort to you, knowing I was there.

Pause.

I am there for you, you know.

CALLUM. I know.

Pause.

SEPHY. This is growing up, I guess, isn't it?

CALLUM. I think it is.

SEPHY. Would you put your arm around me, please?

Pause.

If you'd rather not . . .

CALLUM. No, it's not that.

Pause.

It's just . . . Never mind.

CALLUM *puts his arm around* SEPHY. *She puts her head on his shoulder. They watch the sea.*

Scene Seventeen

Callum's Living Room.

CALLUM (*to audience*). Lynette's funeral was over three months
ago now, and Dad wasn't the only one who'd changed. Most
nights Mum had taken to going for walks, returning long after
I'd gone to bed and was meant to be asleep. Crossmas had
come and gone in our house without much cheer. The new
year had started and here we all were, occupying opposite ends
of the compass. And on top of that, Jude and Dad were somewhere I wasn't wanted . . .

JUDE *and* RYAN *study a map in silence.* MEGGIE *puts her
coat on.* CALLUM *watches.*

MEGGIE. I'm going out.

RYAN. Where?

MEGGIE. For a walk.

RYAN. Meggie, how much longer are you going to carry on
like this?

MEGGIE. Like what?

RYAN. Why won't you talk to me?

MEGGIE. Will you give that up?

RYAN. No.

MEGGIE. Then we have nothing to say to each other.

MEGGIE *leaves the room in disgust.*

RYAN. Meggie . . .

The door slams behind her.

CALLUM. What's going on, Dad?

RYAN. Come on, Jude, we've got work to do.

CALLUM. Where're you going?

RYAN. Out.

CALLUM. Out where?

RYAN. To a meeting.

JUDE. Dad.

CALLUM. What meeting?

RYAN. None of your business.

CALLUM. Where is it?

JUDE. That's none of your business either.

CALLUM. How come Jude gets to go with you and I don't?

RYAN. Because you're not old enough.

CALLUM. Please let me come with you.

JUDE. No way.

CALLUM. I won't be any trouble.

JUDE. Yeah, right!

Pause.

RYAN. Callum, you're not coming with us.

CALLUM. Why not? If Jude's old enough to join the Liberation
    Militia then so am I.

Beat.

RYAN. I don't know what Jude's been telling you, son, but you
    shouldn't believe everything you hear.

CALLUM. I worked it out for myself. I'm not stupid. Besides,
    you haven't exactly been brilliant at hiding it.

Pause.

JUDE. I didn't say anything, Dad, I swear.

RYAN. Callum, you must promise me never to mention this to
    anyone.

CALLUM. Okay.

RYAN. 'Okay' isn't good enough. This could cost us our lives.

CALLUM. I swear I won't tell anyone.

JUDE. You'd better not. That includes your Dagger friend.

Pause.

CALLUM. So can I come with you now?

RYAN. We're going to a meeting and you're way too young. Besides, if you were seen it'd be the end of your school career. Is that what you want?

CALLUM. I don't care. I'm just wasting my time at Heathcroft and everyone knows it. Colin's dropped out and Shania's been expelled for no reason and everyone's taking bets on how long I'm going to last. Besides, I was thinking of leaving anyway.

RYAN. Over my dead body. You are going to school and you'll stay at school until you're eighteen and then you'll go on to university. Do I make myself clear?

Pause.

Callum, I asked you a question. You will not leave school without any qualifications. Understand?

CALLUM. Yeah, okay, okay.

JUDE *and* RYAN *go out.*

Scene Eighteen

The School Corridor.

SEPHY (*to audience*). I started watching people – Noughts and Crosses. Their faces, their body language, the way they spoke to their own kind. The way they spoke to others. And there were so many differences, they swamped the similarities.

Noughts relaxed around each other in a way they rarely did around Crosses. And Crosses were constantly on their guard when near Noughts. Bags got clutched tighter, footsteps quickened, voices grew bigger and brusquer. All our lives crisscrossing but never really touching. A world full of strangers living with all that fear. Nothing was a given any more. Not my life. Not theirs. Nothing.

Scene Nineteen

Callum's House.

CALLUM (*to audience*). Saturday. Eighteen days and five months after Lynette's death. My sixteenth birthday in February had come and gone, with a card and book signed from Mum and Dad, but bought and wrapped by Mum. The winter had passed and spring had arrived but, God, I missed Lynette. I missed her so much.

He picks up the phone and dials. The phone rings three times and he puts down the receiver. He waits. The phone rings back. SEPHY appears on the other side of the stage.

Hello, you.

SEPHY. Hello yourself. Code still working then?

CALLUM. So, what're you up to today?

SEPHY. I'm going shopping. With Mother!

CALLUM. Poor you.

SEPHY. It's not funny.

CALLUM. Of course not.

SEPHY. You're laughing at me again.

CALLUM. As if.

SEPHY. What are you going to do with the rest of the day then?

CALLUM. I thought I might go to the park, or maybe the beach. Perhaps I'll do both. I haven't decided yet.

SEPHY. That's right, rub it in.

CALLUM. Just think of all that lovely money you're going to spend.

SEPHY. Mother's going to spend it, not me. She's decided she needs some retail therapy.

CALLUM. Well, if you can't get out of it, get into it.

SEPHY. I'd much rather be with you.

Pause.

Hello?

CALLUM. Maybe we can meet up later this afternoon.

SEPHY. I doubt it. Mum wants to buy me some dresses and update my school uniform and buy herself an evening gown and some shoes. Just the shoes themselves will take three or four hours at least. I swear, Callum, it's going to be torture.

CALLUM. I might see you at the shopping centre, actually. I've got to get some things for school.

SEPHY. Like what?

CALLUM. I was thinking of buying myself a new calculator.

SEPHY. I'll keep my eyes open for you. Maybe I'll see you at the café. You can stop me from going completely insane.

CALLUM. If I miss you at the centre, how about getting together this evening then? We could have a late picnic on the beach.

SEPHY. I'll try but I can't guarantee anything.

CALLUM. Fair enough.

SEPHY. Saturday in the Dundale Shopping Centre. Just shoot me now and put me out of my misery.

CALLUM (*to audience*). Lunch that Saturday passed without too much grief – for once. Jude had come home from heaven knows where, so we'd all eaten together which made a change.

CALLUM *puts his knife and fork down as if he's finished his meal*.

I'm off.

MEGGIE. Where are you going?

CALLUM. The shopping centre.

JUDE. You can't.

CALLUM. I'll go where I ruddy like. Since when is it any of your business where I go?

RYAN. Callum, I don't want you to go there. Not today.

MEGGIE. What's going on?

CALLUM. Why shouldn't I?

Pause.

What's wrong with going to the shopping centre?

RYAN. I forbid you to go there, Callum.

CALLUM. But –

MEGGIE. What's going on?

CALLUM *clicks*.

JUDE. Callum –

CALLUM (*to audience*). I didn't need to hear any more. I ran out of the house, leaving the front door open.

Scene Twenty

Café at the Dundale Shopping Centre. Cheesy shopping-mall music in the background.

SEPHY (*to audience*). Mother was driving me nuts! In our five long, long hours together, I'd bitten my tongue so many times it'd swollen up to the size of a football. If she asked me for my opinion on one more pair of shoes, I couldn't be responsible for my actions. I sipped my orange juice, grateful for the time alone. She'd gone back to the car park to pack away her various purchases. She was enjoying herself. I'm glad one of us was!

CALLUM *charges in.*

CALLUM. Sephy! You've got to get out of here.

SEPHY. Callum! Where did you spring from?

CALLUM. Never mind that. You've got to leave this place. Now.

SEPHY. But I haven't finished my drink.

CALLUM. Never mind your ruddy drink. You have to leave. Right now.

SEPHY. What's going on?

CALLUM. Don't argue. Out! Come on!

An elderly Cross MAN approaches.

MAN. Excuse me, love, but is this boy troubling you?

SEPHY. No! No. He's a friend of mine. He wants to show me something.

CALLUM *drags* SEPHY *out. A loud alarm goes off.*

What's going on?

CALLUM. Move it. Come on.

SEPHY (*to audience*). We ran towards the nearest exit. We stumbled out into the spring sunshine and still Callum had hold of my hand and was pulling me after him.

CALLUM. Run. Come on.

SEPHY. Where are we going?

CALLUM. Thank God. It took me almost half an hour to find you. Quick.

SEPHY. Callum, I'm getting a stitch.

CALLUM. Tough. We've got to keep going.

SEPHY. Callum, enough!

She pulls her hand out of his. Suddenly there's a huge explosion. We see SHOPPERS *blown in all directions.* SEPHY *and* CALLUM *land near one another. When this is over we hear the sound of sirens.*

CALLUM. Are you okay? You're not hurt?

SEPHY. You knew that was going to happen. You didn't. Tell me you didn't . . .

CALLUM. Let's get you somewhere safe.

SEPHY. Mother! Oh my God!

CALLUM. Sephy!

SEPHY (*to audience*). I jumped to my feet and raced towards the car park across the street from the shopping centre. I was almost there when I remembered Callum. But he was gone.

Scene Twenty-One

Callum's House.

CALLUM (*to audience*). Before I knew where I was, I was face to face with Mum.

MEGGIE. Where have you been? You look terrible. Where's Jude?

CALLUM. I thought he was here.

MEGGIE. He and your dad left straight after you. I thought you were all together. You're shaking.

CALLUM. Haven't you heard?

MEGGIE. Heard what?

CALLUM *picks up the remote and clicks the TV on. The* REPORTER *comes into the room. A live newsflash. He talks to* MEGGIE *and* CALLUM.

REPORTER. . . . At least seven people are known to have been killed outright, with scores more wounded. Casualties are being taken by ground and air ambulances to local hospitals. The wife and daughter of Deputy Prime Minister Kamal Hadley were reported to have been in the shopping centre at the time but are said to be free from injury.

MEGGIE. You were with Persephone, weren't you?

CALLUM. I wanted to buy a new calculator.

REPORTER. A warning was received from the Liberation Militia only five minutes before the bomb actually exploded. We have live images from the scene.

The REPORTER *leads* MEGGIE *and* CALLUM *around* BOMB-INJURY VICTIMS *and* RESCUE WORKERS.

Moments ago, Kamal Hadley spoke to one of our reporters . . .

KAMAL *comes into the room, with a* MINDER *holding an umbrella over him and his* ENTOURAGE.

KAMAL. If the Liberation Militia think this cowardly, barbaric act of terrorism is going to win over the population of this country to their way of thinking, then they are very much mistaken. All they've done is strengthen our resolve not to give in to such people or tactics.

KAMAL *and* ENTOURAGE *leave*.

REPORTER. A senior police officer on the scene promised that the perpetrators would be brought to swift justice. There will be more information about this in our main news bulletin after the current –

We hear the front door open. RYAN *and* JUDE *enter.*
MEGGIE *turns off the TV.*

RYAN. What's for supper?

MEGGIE. I'm going to ask you something, Ryan, and I want
your solemn promise that you're going to tell me the truth.

RYAN. Not now, Meggie.

He moves to exit into the house. MEGGIE *blocks his way.*

MEGGIE. Yes. Now. Were you and Jude involved in planting
that bomb?

RYAN. I don't know what you're talking about.

MEGGIE. Damn it, Ryan, don't treat me like an idiot.

Pause.

RYAN. What I did or didn't do is none of your business.

MEGGIE. Jude, did you plant that bomb?

JUDE *looks at* RYAN.

NO! Don't look at your father. I asked you a question. Now
answer it.

RYAN. Jude, keep your mouth shut, d'you hear?

MEGGIE. I'm still your mother, Jude. Answer me, please.

JUDE. We –

RYAN. Jude!

MEGGIE. Seven people have been killed.

RYAN. What?

CALLUM. It was on the news.

JUDE *looks at* RYAN. JUDE *picks up the remote.* MEGGIE
takes it from him.

MEGGIE. Someone better tell me what's going on because we're
not leaving this room until I know the truth.

JUDE. They were supposed to give a warning.

MEGGIE. Oh my God.

JUDE. They told us no one would be hurt.

MEGGIE. This isn't happening.

JUDE. That everyone would be evacuated.

MEGGIE. You killed – You murdered all those people.

JUDE. Something must have gone wrong.

MEGGIE *is trying to stop herself from retching.*

RYAN. No, son, I reckon they planned it this way.

MEGGIE *hits* RYAN. *She continues to hit him as she speaks.*

MEGGIE. Ryan, you promised me there'd never be anything like this. You promised you'd only be involved in the background. You promised.

RYAN (*restraining her*). I didn't have any choice. Once you're in, they've got you. And you have to do as you're told.

MEGGIE. You don't. You could've said no. You should've said no.

RYAN. Believe me, I had to do it. I had no choice. I was protecting you, Meggie. And our sons.

MEGGIE. Protecting us from what? From something you inflicted on us in the first place. You chose to join them.

RYAN. Who do you think I'm doing all this for?

MEGGIE. I know exactly who you're doing it for. But she's dead, Ryan. And murdering innocent people won't bring her back.

RYAN. You've got it wrong, Meggie.

MEGGIE. Have I? I warned you, Ryan. I begged you not to involve Jude in all this.

CALLUM. I'm sure Dad's sorry. Aren't you, Dad? You didn't mean to hurt those people.

MEGGIE. Sorry? Well, he can say that to the families of all those people he's murdered.

RYAN. We were told there'd be a warning.

MEGGIE. And what if they hadn't? Would you have refused to be involved then?

Silence.

I can't bear to look at you.

Pause.

RYAN. They were legitimate targets.

MEGGIE. All those people killed and maimed, and that's what you have to offer.

RYAN. How many millions of Nought lives have been destroyed by the Crosses over the centuries? No number of people killed in a shopping centre can ever pay for that.

MEGGIE. These are human beings you're talking about.

RYAN. We're in a state of war, Meggie, and it wasn't the Noughts who started it.

MEGGIE. You've been brainwashed.

RYAN. No, you're the one who's been brainwashed. By the telly and the radio and the newspapers. It's all right for them to use violence when they please, to keep us in poverty and bleed us dry. But when we fight back, they call us cowardly and barbaric.

MEGGIE. And what about the Noughts you just killed? It wasn't only Crosses, you know, you killed your own as well.

RYAN. Sometimes the ends have to justify the means. Collateral damage.

Pause.

MEGGIE. In that case we have nothing more to say to each other. I want you out of this house. I want you out of this house by morning.

CALLUM. Mum, please.

RYAN. I'm damned if I'll leave my own house.

MEGGIE. I am not going to let you drag a noose round Jude's neck.

RYAN. I love Jude. That's why I'm in the LM. I want something better for our sons.

MEGGIE. I'm not arguing with you, Ryan. Just pack your bags and go.

CALLUM. Let's leave it now. Let's talk it through tomorrow.

JUDE. If Dad goes, then so do I.

CALLUM. For God's sake, Jude.

RYAN. No you won't.

JUDE. But you can't stop me belonging to the Liberation Militia. I'm not going to bow out now.

MEGGIE. Jude, you're a child. You don't know anything.

JUDE. Mum, for the first time ever I'm part of something. I'm actually doing something I can believe in. And I'm not about to give it up. I'm sorry, but if you send Dad away I'll just go with him.

RYAN. And if I don't take you?

JUDE. Then I'll find somewhere else to stay. But I'm not giving up the LM. I'm not.

MEGGIE. Then you can both leave.

CALLUM. Please, Mum, don't.

MEGGIE. I'll do whatever I have to do to protect Callum. If I can only save one of my children, then so be it.

RYAN. Meggie –

MEGGIE. I don't want you anywhere near me. Don't you ever come near me again.

Exit MEGGIE.

RYAN. Meggie.

RYAN *follows* MEGGIE *off*.

JUDE *looks at* CALLUM. *He exits*.

CALLUM *is left alone. He looks up at the ceiling. He hugs himself.*

Lights fade.

End of Act One.

ACT TWO

Scene One

Sephy's House. The TV room.

SEPHY *enters. She holds a TV remote. She introduces her mother and sister to the audience. There is an empty chair.*

SEPHY (*to audience*). My parents' country house. Seven bed-
rooms and five reception rooms for four people. What a
waste. Four lonely peas rolling about in a cup. More a
museum than a home – all cold floors and marble pillars and
carved stonework. Mother; All she ever did was read glossy
magazines and drink. Spend time in the gym or the pool and
drink. Shop and drink. Every time Mother looked at me, I
could feel her wishing that I was more like my scabby big
sister, Minerva. I called her Minnie for short when I wanted to
annoy her. I called her Minnie all the time. (*She goes to the
empty chair.*) Dad? Dad had found someone else. Her name
was Grace and after the next election he was going to make it
officially known that he and Mum were no longer together.
My family!

SEPHY *flicks the TV on. The* REPORTER *enters.*

REPORTER. Today, Ryan McGregor of Hugo Yard, Meadowview,
was formally charged with Political Terrorism and seven counts
of murder for the bombing outrage at the Dundale Shopping
Centre. He has confessed to all charges. His family are said to
be in hiding.

MINERVA. Blanker scumbag!

SEPHY *flicks the TV off. The* REPORTER *exits.*

SEPHY. Shut it, Minnie.

MINERVA. How many times do I have to tell you not to call me
Minnie? My name is Minerva. M-I-N-E-R-V-A! MINERVA!

SEPHY. Yes, Minnie.

MINERVA. His whole Blanker family should swing, not just him.

JASMINE. Minerva, I won't have language like that in this house, d'you hear? You don't live in Meadowview.

MINERVA. Yes, Mother.

Pause.

And to think we've had him here, in this very house. And Meggie actually used to be our nanny. If the press put two and two together, they're going to have a field day – and Dad's going to have kittens.

SEPHY. What do you mean?

MINERVA. Oh, Sephy, use your brain. If Ryan McGregor gets off, Dad will be accused of favouritism and protecting his own and all sorts, whether or not it has anything to do with him. And you haven't helped things by being his son's little lovebird.

SEPHY. Say what you like, I know those deaths weren't down to Callum's dad.

MINERVA. Nonsense. He's confessed, hasn't he?

SEPHY. Who knows what they did to get that confession out of him.

MINERVA. Get the message, dur-brain. He's a terrorist, end of!

SEPHY. Shut it, Minnie.

MINERVA. Your boyfriend's family are terrorists. Not a very good judge of character, are we?

SEPHY. Mother, they won't really hang him, will they?

JASMINE. If they prove he intended to kill those people, yes.

SEPHY. But I know he didn't, Mum. I know him. He's not capable of it.

MINERVA. And Callum goes to our school. Dad's going to get it in the neck for that as well.

SEPHY. Callum has absolutely nothing to do with this.

MINERVA. An apple never falls far from the tree.

SEPHY. What a pile of –

JASMINE. Persephone!

SEPHY. Even if Ryan McGregor is found guilty – which I don't believe for one second – that doesn't mean that Callum –

JASMINE. Oh, Persephone. Grow up. You're fifteen now. It's about time you stopped behaving like a child!

JASMINE *goes out with her drink.*

SEPHY. Who put a bee in her knickers?

MINERVA. You haven't a clue about the real world, have you?

SEPHY. Congratulations. You sound just like Mother.

MINERVA (*goes to leave*). Take a hike, dog breath.

Pause.

SEPHY. Don't go, Minerva.

MINERVA *stops. She turns to* SEPHY.

MINERVA. What?

Pause.

SEPHY. Do you ever feel lonely?

MINERVA. Missing your Blanker boyfriend, are you?

SEPHY. Please, Minerva. Don't be like that.

Pause.

I wish Dad was here. He doesn't give a damn about us.

MINERVA. That's not true. Dad cares in his own way.

SEPHY. Just not as much as he cares about his political career. Or Grace.

Pause.

MINERVA. It's not easy for him with Mum's drinking.

SEPHY. Do you think he'll ever come back?

MINERVA. Maybe if Mum changes. Gives up the booze.

SEPHY. Well, that's that then.

Pause.

What are we going to do?

MINERVA. What can we do?

SEPHY. The drinking's getting worse.

MINERVA. She's just smoothing over some of the rough edges.

SEPHY. Any smoother and she's going to slip over and break her neck.

MINERVA. Sephy, if she doesn't want to be helped then there's nothing we can do.

SEPHY. I miss her. The person she used to be.

MINERVA. We all miss her, but this is the way things are. We just have to deal with it.

SEPHY (*to audience*). Maybe Minnie was right. Things are the way they are and one person would never make a difference to a ruddy thing.

Scene Two

Stanhope's Office.

CALLUM (*to audience*). Mum and I were shown into Mr Stanhope's plush office. His secretary had told Mum it was 'urgent' and 'about the case', but Mum and I both had the same question: 'What case?' The last time we'd seen Mr Stanhope, which was only three days ago, he's told us quite categorically that he couldn't take Dad on.

STANHOPE. Mrs McGregor, Callum, please take a seat.

MEGGIE. You have some news? Are they going to let Ryan go?

STANHOPE. I'm afraid not. Your husband still insists that he's guilty.

Pause.

CALLUM. He's not. He only confessed because the police threatened to imprison the lot of us. Dad didn't even plant that bomb. I know who did.

STANHOPE. I've been trying to get in touch with you at your home address but there's been no reply.

MEGGIE. We're staying with my sister, Charlotte, on the other side of Meadowview.

STANHOPE. You've been getting hate-letters?

CALLUM (*to audience*). Amongst other things. Like bricks through the window and death threats.

STANHOPE. Well, I'm happy to tell you that I will be able to take on your husband's case. And the really good news is, I've persuaded Kelani Adams QC to act as your barrister – not that she took much persuading.

MEGGIE. I can't afford Kelani Adams.

STANHOPE. Don't worry about that. Her fees are all taken care of.

CALLUM. What does that mean?

STANHOPE. It means that you don't have to worry about the money.

MEGGIE. I'd appreciate it if you answered my son's question properly.

STANHOPE. An anonymous benefactor has stepped forward with a very generous sum of money, to ensure that your husband gets the fairest trial possible.

MEGGIE. We don't take charity, Mr Stanhope.

STANHOPE. It's not charity. I was told to inform you of that in the strongest possible terms.

MEGGIE. By who?

CALLUM. Does it matter, Mum?

STANHOPE. As I said, I received a banker's cheque and a typewritten, unsigned note with several instructions.

MEGGIE. May we see the note?

CALLUM. What's the point?

STANHOPE. I'm afraid not. One of the conditions was that you shouldn't be allowed to see it.

MEGGIE. Well, I'm sorry. We can't accept it.

CALLUM. We can't afford not to.

MEGGIE. How do we know where this money's come from, Callum?

STANHOPE. Mrs McGregor, this is your husband's one and only chance. I would strongly advise you to take it.

MEGGIE. Let me get this straight: the only reason you're still involved in this case is because someone has paid you to stay involved – is that right?

STANHOPE. I have an office to run, Mrs McGregor.

MEGGIE. And the only reason Kelani Adams is involved is because she's being paid a great deal of money – is that right?

STANHOPE. As I understand it, Ms Adams is prepared to take on the case because she believes in it. And she believes she can win it.

MEGGIE. But the money's the only thing that's changed.

CALLUM. Who cares, Mum? Let's just accept the offer and get on with proving that Dad didn't plant that bomb.

STANHOPE. Your agreement is all that will be required.

Pause.

CALLUM. Mum, I think we should do whatever it takes to save Dad's life. It doesn't matter where the money came from. We have to do what we can. We've just got to swallow our pride.

Pause.

MEGGIE. Okay then.

CALLUM (*to audience*). I knew who had sent the money to Mr Stanhope. I had no idea how she'd done it. And I had even less idea how I was ever going to thank her, never mind repay her. But I would. I sat in Mr Stanhope's office, on his expensive brown leather chair, and swore an oath before God that I would pay Sephy back. If it took me every penny I earned for the rest of my life, I would repay her.

Scene Three

Sephy's House.

SEPHY (*to audience*). I came home from school and got the shock of my life. Dad's suitcases were in the hallway.

Enter KAMAL with MINERVA. JASMINE follows, holding a large glass of wine.

KAMAL. Hello, princess.

SEPHY *runs up to* KAMAL *and hugs him.*

SEPHY. Dad! I've missed you.

KAMAL. I've missed you too.

He swings her around.

Good grief! What have you been eating? You weigh a ton!

SEPHY. Thanks a bunch! Are you staying for good?

KAMAL. For a while, at least.

SEPHY *clocks* JASMINE.

SEPHY. What? What's going on?

JASMINE. Ask your father. He has all the answers.

Pause.

SEPHY. Oh, I get it. You're only here for the trial. Aren't you?

Enter MINERVA, *dressed up.*

MINERVA. Ready.

SEPHY. Why are you dressed like that?

Enter JUNO, KAMAL*'s PR.*

JUNO. We thought the front steps would be best. You must be Sephy.

She offers SEPHY *her hand.*

SEPHY. Hello.

JUNO. Juno Aylette, your dad's PR. But we have to get a move on, I'm afraid. The light's fading.

KAMAL. We'll be right out.

JUNO. Great. What beautiful girls. They won't need much in the way of make-up.

SEPHY. What's going on?

KAMAL. Just a quick family photo, princess. Thanks, Juno, we'll be out in a moment.

JUNO. Sure.

JUNO *exits.*

MINERVA. We're going to be in the Sunday papers. How cool is that?

SEPHY. What?

JASMINE. Let's just get it over with.

KAMAL. You'd better get changed, princess.

MINERVA. Something smart, but relaxed.

SEPHY. No way.

KAMAL. Come on, sweetheart. Then we can go out for supper. Celebrate me being home.

SEPHY. I'm not doing it, Dad. I don't care how many times you ask. I'm not going to play 'happy family' for the cameras. You'll have to boost your poll ratings without me.

KAMAL. But they want the whole family, princess.

JUNO *comes back in.*

JUNO. Mr Hadley, the light . . .

MINERVA. Come on, Dad. Let's do it without her.

KAMAL (*to* SEPHY). Suit yourself, young lady.

They go to exit.

Your glass, Jasmine.

JASMINE. Oh.

JUNO, MINERVA *and* KAMAL *exit, leaving* SEPHY. JASMINE *takes a swig of the wine and puts the glass down.*

I don't blame you for not joining in.

KAMAL (*offstage*). Jasmine! Hurry up.

JASMINE *goes.*

SEPHY *looks at the glass of wine. She goes towards it, picks up the glass and sniffs it. She brings it to her lips and takes a long swig. She pauses. Takes another swig, then finishes the glass.*

Scene Four

Mr Corsa's Office, Heathcroft School.

CALLUM (*to audience*). I'd seen a lot of plush offices this week. First Mr Stanhope, now Mr Corsa, our headmaster. Stepping onto his carpet felt like walking on spring grass.

CALLUM *sits*.

MR CORSA. Callum, there's no easy way to say this, so I'm going to get right to the point.

CALLUM. Yes, sir?

MR CORSA. Until the matter regarding your father is satisfactorily resolved, the governors and I have decided that it would serve everyone's best interests if you were suspended for a while.

CALLUM. I'm guilty till my dad's proven innocent? Is that it?

MR CORSA. Callum, I do hope you're going to be reasonable about this.

CALLUM. Should I empty my locker now or will the end of the day be soon enough?

MR CORSA. That's entirely up to you.

CALLUM. You must be delighted. Two down, only one more to go.

MR CORSA. Meaning?

CALLUM. Meaning, Colin has gone and you couldn't wait to get rid of Shania and now it's my turn.

MR CORSA. Shania was expelled for gross misconduct.

CALLUM. Shania only slapped Gardner Wilson because he hit her first. And everyone knows that, including you. How come Shania gets expelled and Gardner gets away with a telling off? Why isn't it gross misconduct when a Cross does it?

MR CORSA. I have no intention of justifying school policy to you. We'll be happy to review your situation once the trial is over and the dust clears.

CALLUM. But the dust is never going to clear, is it? And we both know that.

MR CORSA *holds out his hand*. CALLUM *looks at it*.

MR CORSA. Good luck to you, Callum.

CALLUM (*to audience*). I turned back and slammed the door as hard as I could. A childish gesture, I know. But it felt so good.

MR CORSA. Callum, come here!

CALLUM (*to audience*). I carried on walking.

MR CORSA. I said, come back here.

CALLUM (*to audience*). I wasn't part of his school any more. I didn't have to do what he said. I wasn't part of the whole Cross way of life. Why should I do what any of them said? I was out of Heathcroft. And I was never coming back.

Scene Five

Sephy's House.

SEPHY (*to audience*). I limit myself to one glass a night. I don't like the taste particularly. But it makes me feel better. Kind of warm and careless. It smoothes out the rough edges. I don't mind so much about Mother or Father or Minerva any more. I don't even mind about Callum. A couple of drinks and I don't mind about anything. Isn't that cool?

Scene Six

The Trial.

CALLUM (*to audience*). When they brought me into the court-room I could see my father to the right. The judge was droning on and on at the jury, telling them what the case was about and what it was not about. Twelve good men and women and true. Twelve good Cross men and women, of course. How else could justice be served? I looked down at the Good Book under my hand. It was cool, almost cold beneath my fingers. The truth? Which version of the truth will this Cross court find acceptable?

MR PINGULE *enters*.

MR PINGULE. Callum, what's your opinion of the Liberation Militia?

CALLUM. I . . . Any organisation which promotes equality between Noughts and Crosses is . . . Noughts and Crosses should be equal . . . I support anyone who tries to bring that about.

MR PINGULE. So neither you or anyone in your family knew anything about the planting of the bomb at the Dundale Shopping Centre?

CALLUM. No.

MR PINGULE. Well, can you tell me what you were doing in the Dundale approximately ten minutes before the bomb went off?

CALLUM (*to audience*). I watched as a TV with a massive screen and a VCR were wheeled into the court.

MR PINGULE. In this film, who are you pulling from the Cuckoo's Egg Café?

CALLUM. Sephy.

MR PINGULE. Sorry, what was that?

CALLUM. Persephone Hadley.

MR PINGULE. What is your relationship with Persephone Hadley?

CALLUM. She's . . . she's a friend.

MR PINGULE. Could you tell me why you were in such a hurry to get Persephone out of the Dundale Shopping Centre, just before the bomb went off?

CALLUM. I was late and I was afraid her mum would appear at any second and . . . I wanted to show her something.

MR PINGULE. What was that?

CALLUM. Something silly.

Pause.

With everything that's happened, I can't remember.

MR PINGULE. No further questions.

MR PINGULE *exits*.

CALLUM (*to audience*). Forgive me, Dad, please forgive me.

SEPHY (*to audience*). I don't know how Callum's mum managed to get Kelani Adams to defend Mr McGregor, but I was so glad she had. Even I'd heard of Kelani Adams. According to the telly, Kelani was making sure that the trial was as fair as possible.

KELANI ADAMS *enters*.

KELANI. Could you describe your relationship with Mrs Hadley, Persephone Hadley's mother?

CALLUM. Mrs Hadley . . . doesn't much like me.

KELANI. Callum, what would you have done if Persephone had been in the café with her mother?

CALLUM (*to audience*). How should I answer? Think! Think!

KELANI. Yes, Callum?

CALLUM. I would have waited until Sephy was alone before trying to speak to her.

KELANI. But it might have taken a while before you got to tell Sephy what you wanted to tell her?

CALLUM. Yes.

KELANI. Is that why you were in such a hurry?

CALLUM. It was.

KELANI. Thank you, Callum. That will be all.

KELANI *exits*.

SEPHY (*to audience*). Ryan McGregor just had to be found Not Guilty. It was only right and proper.

CALLUM (*to audience*). Good or bad, every aspect of my life lay in the hands of others. Kelani Adams, the teachers at Heathcroft, now the jury.

SEPHY (*to audience*). Ryan wasn't guilty. So why did I feel like I was the only person in the world – the only Cross in the world – to believe that?

CALLUM (*to audience*). Maybe this was it. Maybe this was all there was or would ever be to my life.

SEPHY (*to audience*). But justice simply had to be done. The jury would see the truth.

CALLUM (*to audience*). Mum and I held hands as we waited for the foreman to speak. Hope and hopelessness churned in my stomach like oil and water.

Enter CLERK OF COURT.

CLERK. D'you find the defendant, Ryan McGregor, Guilty or Not Guilty of the crime of Political Terrorism?

CALLUM (*to audience*). Why was the foreman taking so long to speak? Answer the question . . . What's your answer? Why couldn't I hear anything?

CLERK. Do you find the defendant, Ryan McGregor, Guilty or Not Guilty of the crime of First-Degree Murder?

CALLUM (*to audience*). And I heard the verdict that time. God help me, I heard it.

Scene Seven

Sephy's Garden.

SEPHY (*to audience*). I sat on the garden swing. I didn't actually swing any more – that was kid's stuff. I just . . . twisted. I'd come home and gone straight out into the garden. For the two weeks after the trial, Mother had got worse, so now I just did what I was told and kept my head down. And for the most part it worked.

JASMINE (*offstage*). Sephy, what are you doing?

SEPHY (*to audience*). Uh-oh! Trouble!

JASMINE. Come here, please.

SEPHY (*to audience*). I jumped off the swing and ran into the house.

Enter JASMINE.

JASMINE. Go to your room and put on your navy-blue dress and your blue shoes.

SEPHY. My Jackson Spacey?

JASMINE. Be downstairs in five minutes. We need to be on our way by half past four.

SEPHY. Where are we going?

JASMINE. Never you mind.

SEPHY. Why do I have to get dressed up?

JASMINE. Because I said so. Do as you're told. And tell your sister to hurry up as well.

SEPHY. But why?

JASMINE. Just get a move on, please.

As she changes into the dress she wore at Lynette's funeral.

SEPHY (*to audience*). I knew it was something major when Dad was standing in the driveway next to his official government Mercedes. I hadn't seen him since the trial finished. Ten to six and our car drew up outside Hewmett Prison. And only then, when it'd been spelt out for me, did I finally realise what I was doing there.

Scene Eight

The Prison. The execution chamber.

A gallows. CALLUM *and family,* SEPHY *and family. A* CROWD OF NOUGHTS *on one side and* CROWD OF CROSSES *on the other.*

The REPORTER *is also present and taking notes.*

CLERK. Ladies and Gentlemen and Noughts, we are here today to witness the execution of Ryan McGregor of 15 Hugo Yard, Meadowview, having been found guilty of seven counts of murder and the charge of political terrorism. The sentence will now be carried out of hanging by the neck until he is dead.

SEPHY (*to audience*). I didn't know, Callum.

CLERK. Bring in the prisoner.

A GUARD *brings* RYAN *in.* SEPHY *looks at* CALLUM.

SEPHY (*to audience*). How to make my desperate thoughts reach him? I swear I didn't know, Callum. I wouldn't have come if I'd known where we were going. Wild horses couldn't have dragged me through those gates. That's the truth. Callum, you must believe that.

CLERK (*to* RYAN). Do you have anything to say?

SEPHY. Mother, I want to leave.

RYAN shakes his head. An EXECUTIONER *covers his head with a hood.*

JASMINE. Not now, Sephy.

SEPHY (*standing*). I want to leave – NOW.

JASMINE. Sit down, Persephone, and stop making an exhibition of yourself.

SEPHY. Nothing is going to make me sit here and watch this. I'm leaving.

She goes to leave. JASMINE *grabs her.*

JASMINE. Now sit down and don't say another word.

SEPHY *sits down*.

The prison clock chimes four times. On the fifth:

RYAN. Long live the Liberation Militia!

The PRISON GOVERNOR *enters*.

GOVERNOR. Wait! Wait!

The clock strikes six.

Ladies and Gentlemen and Noughts, I am Governor Giustini. I have just been informed that Ryan McGregor has received a reprieve. His sentence has been commuted to life imprisonment.

RYAN. Long live the . . .

RYAN *collapses but is caught by the* GUARD *and led out*.

The NOUGHTS *riot under:*

CALLUM (*to audience*). We could have torn down Hewmett Prison brick by brick. We would've. I turned to where they were sitting. I couldn't see her. Where was she? Watching all this and enjoying the free entertainment. At that precise moment I felt like I could rip the metal barriers out of the concrete beneath my feet with my bare hands. Someone grabbed my arm. It was Mum. And just like that, all my anger subsided. I stood watching Mum. Waiting for the pain inside to dampen down. Waiting for the world around me to turn multicoloured again. Instead of blood red.

The HADLEYS *leave. The* CROWD *melt away*.

Scene Nine

Sephy's House. The kitchen.

JASMINE *pours herself a glass of wine from a Chardonnay bottle.*

SEPHY (*to* JASMINE). Don't you ever, ever do that to me again!

JASMINE. Calm down, please, young lady.

SEPHY. How could you take me to that . . . thing? How could you?

JASMINE. We didn't have a choice. It was our duty.

SEPHY. Our duty? To sit and watch a man get hanged?

JASMINE. Yes. We have a duty to support your father, whether we agree with what he's doing or not.

SEPHY. That was . . . barbaric. Taking us to watch a man die. Dad's sick. So are you.

JASMINE. I didn't like it any more than you did.

SEPHY. Liar. You couldn't take your eyes off it.

JASMINE. I couldn't even look.

> *As* JASMINE *goes to pour another glass of wine.* SEPHY *snatches the half-empty bottle from her.*

> Give me that bottle.

SEPHY. Or what?

JASMINE. Persephone, give me that bottle. Now.

> SEPHY *throws the bottle across the floor and it smashes.*

> Go to your room.

SEPHY. You couldn't care less, could you? You would have cared more if they were hanging a wine bottle instead of a person.

> JASMINE *slaps* SEPHY.

JASMINE. How dare you speak to me like that?

SEPHY. There's wine spilling out over there. Go and lick it up then. You wouldn't want to waste any, would you?

Pause.

Waiting for me to leave before you get on your hands and knees? Okay then. I'll leave you to it.

JASMINE *grabs* SEPHY *and turns her round.*

JASMINE. You don't know every damn thing, Persephone. You think you're the only one in pain here? Ryan McGregor was my friend. So was Meggie. Do you think I wanted to watch him hang?

SEPHY. You still went.

JASMINE. One day you'll realise that you can't always do what you want in this life. And when you realise that, maybe you'll stop judging me.

SEPHY. I want to think of you as little as possible.

JASMINE. Oh, grow up.

SEPHY. You say they were your friends? Nothing would make me go to the hanging of one of my friends. Nothing. Not even Dad.

JASMINE. I tried to help.

SEPHY. How? By getting drunk?

JASMINE. Who d'you think paid for all their legal fees, you stupid girl?

Pause.

SEPHY. I don't believe you.

JASMINE. I did everything that was humanly possible to make sure Ryan McGregor wouldn't hang. And that's not to leave this room.

Pause.

SEPHY. If you did, it was only because of your guilty conscience. You've never done anything for another human being in your life.

JASMINE. Well, I brought you and your sister up.

SEPHY. No, that was Meggie McGregor.

JASMINE. Meggie McGregor looked after you because she was paid. And paid well. Maybe, when you have a daughter of your own, you'll find out that being a mother is not as easy as it seems. Life can be very cruel and very lonely and it would be nice, once in a while, to be treated with a degree of respect.

Pause.

SEPHY. Oh, go back to your bottle. You deserve each other.

SEPHY *runs to her room and gets out a bottle of alcohol. She takes the lid off and goes to drink it. She stops. She throws the bottle away. At the same time, we see* JASMINE *clearing up the mess from the kitchen floor.*

Scene Ten

The Prison. The visiting room.

CALLUM (*to audience*). Two hours and a lot of arguing from our solicitor later, we were finally allowed into the visiting room to see Dad.

OFFICER. You've got five minutes.

RYAN. I hear they're blaming me for the riot.

MEGGIE. How are you?

Pause.

Well, at least we can be grateful for the reprieve.

RYAN. They should have hanged me. It would have been kinder.

MEGGIE. Don't say that.

RYAN. Why not? Do you really think I want to spend the rest of my life locked up in this hellhole?

KELANI *enters*.

KELANI. We've won the first battle. Onto the next one. I've already launched the appeal.

RYAN. With all due respect, Miss Adams, this is as far as you'll get.

KELANI. Oh no it's not. I'm calling in every favour I'm owed.

RYAN. I don't want to appeal, Miss Adams, I haven't got the strength. I think that we both know that I'll never see the outside of this prison again.

Pause.

MEGGIE. That's not true.

Pause.

KELANI. You need some time to think it over.

RYAN. The only way I'm leaving this place is in a box. Hopefully sooner rather than later.

MEGGIE. For God's sake, Ryan. Callum's here.

KELANI. I'll come back in a few days, see how you're feeling then.

RYAN. I won't feel any different.

CALLUM. Please think about it, Dad.

RYAN. How's school, son?

Pause.

CALLUM. It's fine, Dad. All fine.

RYAN. That's great news. You make sure you get good results.

CALLUM. I'll do my best.

RYAN. I'm very proud of you, son.

OFFICER. That's it. Visiting time is over.

MEGGIE. See you next week, love.

CALLUM. Bye, Dad.

RYAN. I'm expecting A's, Callum. Straight A's.

OFFICER *removes* RYAN.

KELANI. I'm sure he'll come round. It's quite natural to feel despondent after what he's been through.

MEGGIE. He didn't even say goodbye.

Scene Eleven

Sephy's House. The dining room.

SEPHY (*to audience*). The night the TV showed Callum's house burned to the ground, I went to my bedroom and cried and cried. I wanted to phone but I didn't have his new number. I wanted to visit but I didn't have his new address. I still went to the beach once in a while but he was never there. I pretended to myself that we just kept missing each other. I'd arrive at five, he'd arrive at six. I'd arrive at six, he'd arrive at seven. But deep down I knew that he'd stopped coming. He had more important things on his mind. When the trial ended, I went back to seeing more of Dad on the telly than I did in the flesh. I suspected something fishy was going on when, one day, his car pulled up outside the house in time for dinner.

SEPHY, MINERVA, KAMAL *and* JASMINE *sit at dinner. They eat in silence.*

KAMAL. So, how's school going, princess?

SEPHY (*to audience*). 'Princess'? Definitely fishy!

KAMAL. Mother tells me your results have been good.

SEPHY. Heathcroft's fine, Dad. Fairly boring, actually.

KAMAL. I worry sometimes that Heathcroft doesn't quite stretch you enough.

SEPHY. It's a good school. Loads of people move here to get their kids in.

KAMAL. Look, I'm concerned – your mother and I are concerned – about how things will go for you there, now that Ryan McGregor's been convicted.

SEPHY. Why would things be bad for me? Why would they be worse for me than for Minerva?

KAMAL. I think we all know why.

SEPHY. I'm afraid my telepathic powers aren't what they used to be.

JASMINE. Please don't be cheeky, Persephone.

KAMAL. Look, when you were attacked by those girls, it happened because of your friendship with the McGregor boy.

SEPHY. It happened because those girls were ignorant bigots. And his name's Callum. Anyway, you don't need to worry about him, they've booted him out along with the other Noughts who dared to believe they were entitled to a decent education.

KAMAL. We think it would be better if we took you out of Heathcroft. We've made enquiries at Chivers. They have a place and they could take you in next term.

SEPHY. But I don't want to go to boarding school. I like it at Heathcroft.

KAMAL. Your mother and I are in complete agreement on this. Aren't we, Jasmine?

Pause.

Jasmine?

JASMINE. It's all for the best, darling. And Chivers is one of the finest schools in the country.

SEPHY. So what? This has nothing to do with my education. You're just frightened that the TV and the ruddy newspapers will find out that Meggie used to work for us. As usual, it's about your ruddy career.

JASMINE. Watch your language, young lady.

KAMAL. I want to get you away from the McGregors and everything they stand for.

SEPHY. But Callum had nothing to do with Dundale. It's his father that's been convicted, not him.

KAMAL. That won't matter to the thugs, princess. They know you as a friend of the McGregors. I trust you saw what they did to his house.

MINERVA. He's thinking about you, Sephy.

SEPHY. You won't make me go. I'll refuse. I'll leave home and move in with Callum.

KAMAL. You do that and I'll cut you off without a penny.

SEPHY. I couldn't care less. We'll go away together. Go up north. Start a new life.

KAMAL. How will you pay for that?

SEPHY. I'll work.

KAMAL. I'm afraid we've made the decision and we're not going to change our minds. In September, you're going to Chivers and that's the end of it.

He gets up.

JASMINE (*to* KAMAL). You're not leaving now, surely.

KAMAL. The PM's called a security summit.

SEPHY (*to audience*). Dinner with Gracey, more like.

KAMAL. It'll all work out, princess. Trust me.

KAMAL *goes to kiss* SEPHY *on the forehead. She pulls away. He goes to exit.*

JASMINE. Please stay and finish your meal, Kamal. For the girls.

KAMAL. Look, I told her myself. That's what you wanted, wasn't it?

JASMINE. I was hoping you might want to spend some time with your daughters.

KAMAL. I'll see them next week.

JASMINE. When?

KAMAL. I'll have to check my diary.

JASMINE. Perhaps you'd like me to call your secretary. Make an appointment.

KAMAL. If you were sober enough to remember, that might be a good idea.

SEPHY. Send our love to Gracey!

He goes.

JASMINE. I know it's hard for you, darling, but maybe boarding school will be an adventure.

SEPHY. I thought you said you cried yourself to sleep every night when you were there.

JASMINE. Well, I was only eight when I started. At your age it's different. You'll make friends and I'm sure you'll grow to love it.

SEPHY. More to the point, I'll be out of your hair.

JASMINE. You know that's not true, Sephy. I'll miss you terribly.

SEPHY. Good thing Dad's not sending your Chardonnay supplier away. Then you'd be in real trouble.

JASMINE. What a lovely family meal! We really must do it more often.

JASMINE goes.

MINERVA. You ought to lay off her, Sephy. She doesn't need you on her case 24/7.

SEPHY. She can stand up for herself, can't she? She's not a child.

MINERVA. She's incredibly vulnerable right now. Haven't you noticed?

Pause.

You're not seriously thinking of running off with that Blanker.

SEPHY. Just watch me.

MINERVA. You haven't got the nerve.

Scene Twelve

Sephy's Bedroom. Night-time.

The sound of pebbles on a window. SEPHY *goes to her window.*

SEPHY (*to audience*). It must have been two o'clock in the morning. It took a while before I heard the strange tip-tapping at my window. And once I was conscious of it, I realised that it'd been going on for a while. I headed for my balcony window and opened it. Tiny stones lay at my feet.

CALLUM (*offstage*). Sephy!

SEPHY. What? How did you get through security?

CALLUM (*offstage*). I need to see you.

SEPHY. I'll come down. It's safer.

CALLUM (*offstage*). No. I'll climb up.

SEPHY. Hang on, I'll tie some sheets together then.

CALLUM (*offstage*). No, don't bother.

SEPHY (*offstage, as* CALLUM *climbs*). Be quick. The place is crawling with guards. Watch it . . . Mind the living-room window. No. Get your left hand over the balcony. That's it.

CALLUM *enters through the window.*

Did you phone me? I didn't hear your signal.

CALLUM. I was at the prison with my dad.

CALLUM and SEPHY take each other in.

SEPHY. How's your mum?

CALLUM. She's at my aunt's house.

SEPHY goes to her door and locks it.

SEPHY. They're sending me away to boarding school. In September. The thirteenth. Unlucky for some.

CALLUM. Well, that's the end of us, I suppose.

SEPHY. It doesn't have to be.

CALLUM. Come off it, Sephy.

SEPHY. Remember that time on the beach? The night before you started at Heathcroft? You talked about us going away together. Escaping. Remember?

Pause.

Well, how about it? I've taken my savings out of the bank. And we can both work. We could move right away from here. Maybe rent a place up north somewhere. Maybe in the country.

Pause.

CALLUM. Your father must be happy. My dad rots away in prison and just like that, Kamal Hadley's reputation is restored. Is this the way it's going to be from now on? Whenever a politician is in trouble in the polls they'll just search out the nearest Nought to put away or string up – or both? Cheaper than starting a war, I suppose.

SEPHY. I know your dad didn't kill those people.

CALLUM. Do you know how long the jury deliberated? One hour. One lousy stinking hour.

SEPHY touches CALLUM's cheek.

SEPHY. I'm so sorry, Callum.

CALLUM *pulls his head away.*

CALLUM. I don't want your ruddy pity.

SEPHY. Stop it. Please.

CALLUM. Why should I? Don't you want anyone to know YOU'VE GOT A BLANKER IN YOUR ROOM?

SEPHY. Callum, don't.

CALLUM. I want to smash you and every other Dagger who crosses my path. I hate you so much it scares me.

SEPHY. I know you do. You've hated me ever since you joined Heathcroft and I called you a Blanker.

CALLUM. And you've hated me for turning my back on you at school and not being there when you needed me.

Pause.

Then why is it that I think of you as my best friend?

SEPHY. Because you know that's how I think of you. Because I love you. And you love me, I think.

Pause.

Did you hear what I said? I love you.

CALLUM. Love doesn't exist – friendship doesn't exist between a Nought and a Cross.

SEPHY. Then what are you doing in my room?

CALLUM. I'm damned if I know.

SEPHY *sits on the bed.* CALLUM *sits alongside her but some distance away. They are both very uncomfortable. They look at the floor. Then* SEPHY *turns to* CALLUM *and offers her hand. He turns to her. She starts to lower her hand. He takes it and moves towards her. We hear the gentle sound of waves on the beach. They sit like this for a few moments. Then he kicks off his shoes and lies down on the bed, taking her with him. They hug.*

Are you okay?

SEPHY. Uh-hm.

CALLUM. I'm not squashing you?

SEPHY. Uh-uh.

CALLUM. You're sure?

SEPHY. Callum, shut up.

CALLUM smiles.

Callum, I'm sorry I sat at your table.

CALLUM. Forget it. It doesn't matter.

SEPHY. And I'm sorry for what happened at Lynette's funeral.

CALLUM. You only meant to help.

SEPHY turns to face him. They kiss. SEPHY pulls away.

SEPHY. Let's just get some sleep – okay?

CALLUM. Okay.

They curl up.

Sephy.

SEPHY. Mmmm.

CALLUM. Maybe we should go away together.

SEPHY's nodding off.

SEPHY. We'll talk about it in the morning.

Pause.

CALLUM. I remember years ago when you snuck me my first taste of orange juice. It was icy-cold and I'd never tasted anything so sweet and I held each sip in my mouth until it became warm because I couldn't bear to swallow it. I wanted the taste to last for ever.

Silence.

Sephy, I want to tell you something.

Silence.

A secret.

Silence.

Sephy?

He realises she's asleep and gives up. They lie still together. The light slowly fades from night to morning as they sleep. Dawn chorus.

Scene Thirteen

Sephy's Bedroom. Midday.

We hear an offstage knocking at the door. SEPHY *starts to wake up.*

SARAH (*offstage*). Miss Sephy? It's Sarah and your mother. Are you all right in there?

JASMINE (*offstage*). Persephone, open this door. At once.

Another knock.

Persephone, open the door right this second or I'll get security to break it down.

SARAH (*offstage*). Miss Sephy, are you okay? Please.

SEPHY. Just . . . a minute.

She shakes CALLUM *awake.*

CALLUM. What . . . what's the . . . ?

Another knock on the door. SEPHY *puts her hand over* CALLUM's *mouth. She points towards the door. He goes to get under the bed.*

SEPHY (*whispering*). Look, why don't I just let them in? I want my mother to know about us. Besides, we haven't done anything wrong.

CALLUM *looks at her.*

Bad idea?

CALLUM. Dur.

He disappears under the bed. SEPHY *goes to put her dressing gown on over her Jackson Spacey dress. More knocking.*

SEPHY. I'm on my way, Sarah. I'm just putting on my dressing gown.

She rushes off to unlock the door and opens it. JASMINE *rushes past her into the room.* SARAH *follows.* JASMINE *goes to the window and looks out.*

What's the matter? Is the house on fire?

JASMINE. D'you know what time it is?

SEPHY. So I overslept a few minutes. Big deal.

SARAH. It's almost noon and your door is locked.

SEPHY. Maybe I decided to bring a little excitement into your lives.

SEPHY notices CALLUM's hand reaching out from under the bed to retrieve his trainers, which are on SEPHY and SARAH's side of the bed. He grabs a trainer and removes it.

I'll be down as soon as I've had my shower. I promise.

JASMINE. There's nothing wrong?

SEPHY. Course not. What could be wrong?

SARAH turns to leave and notices CALLUM's remaining trainer.

JASMINE. You're hiding something. I know it.

SEPHY. Just 'cause I overslept?

SARAH heads towards the trainer.

Sarah, what?

SARAH surreptitiously kicks the trainer under the bed, then covers her movements by tidying SEPHY's bedclothes.

JASMINE. My daughter is quite capable of making her own bed, Sarah.

SARAH. Yes, Mrs Hadley.

JASMINE goes off to the door and exits. SARAH follows. Just before exiting, she checks to see that JASMINE has cleared, then turns back to SEPHY.

(*Whispering.*) Get Callum dressed and out of here!

She exits and we hear her shutting the door.

SEPHY. You can come out now.

CALLUM sticks his head out and they both burst out laughing.

CALLUM. Just your ordinary average Sunday morning.

SEPHY. Never a dull moment.

CALLUM starts writing something on a piece of paper.

What's that?

CALLUM. The address at my aunt's. You can contact me there. If you're serious about going away, you'll know where to find me. I'd better go.

They kiss. He exits. She gets on the bed and turns on the TV. The REPORTER enters.

REPORTER (*to audience*). Ryan McGregor, the convicted bomber of the Dundale Shopping Centre, was killed this morning whilst trying to escape from Hewmett Prison. He died whilst attempting to scale the electrified fence surrounding the prison. McGregor was due to hang yesterday but received a dramatic last-minute reprieve from the Home Office. His family are said to be devastated at the news and were unavailable for comment. Officials have launched an immediate inquiry. A statement was issued today saying that suicide would not be ruled out as the official cause of death.

SEPHY flicks off the TV and the REPORTER exits.

Scene Fourteen

Sephy's House. Sarah's office.

SEPHY (*to audience*). When Mr McGregor died I didn't contact
Callum. I'd got it so wrong with Lynette that I was frightened
of making the same mistake again. I decided to wait. The
summer passed by in a blur and before long it was the twelfth
of September. The day before I was due to go to Chivers. It
was now or never.

SEPHY puts a letter in an envelope and goes to SARAH.

Morning, Sarah, I . . . Could you do me a favour? A really big
one.

SARAH. Oh yes? What's that then?

SEPHY. Could you deliver this letter to Callum McGregor?
Today? He's staying with his aunt. I've written the address on
the front.

SARAH. I don't think so. I can't afford to lose this job.

SEPHY. Please, Sarah. I'm begging you. It's really important.

Pause.

SARAH. You're not pregnant, are you?

SEPHY laughs.

I guess not.

SEPHY. Please. I wouldn't ask you if it wasn't really, really
important.

SARAH. Okay. I'll deliver it on my way home tonight. But only
on one condition.

SEPHY. What's that?

SARAH. That you don't do anything . . . hasty.

SEPHY. It's a deal.

She hugs SARAH. *SEPHY hands* SARAH *the letter.* SARAH
exits.

(*To audience*.) Hasty? Hasty? I'd thought and considered and planned this for days, weeks, months, all my life. Callum would read my letter and come for me and together we were going to escape. Tomorrow.

Scene Fifteen

Burger Bar.

CALLUM *sits with his drink.*

CALLUM (*to audience*). The days stretched before me like a never-ending desert. They'd killed . . . They'd murdered my dad in July and it was now September. When Dad died, something inside me had died as well. Although the weeks had come and gone, it still cut like a knife every time I thought of him. I hadn't heard from Sephy since the Saturday night and Sunday morning I spent with her. All that talk about running away. Fairy tales. And tomorrow was the day that she was leaving for boarding school. They were right – love doesn't exist between a Nought and a Cross. And it never would.

Enter JUDE *behind* CALLUM.

JUDE. Hello, little brother.

CALLUM. Jude!

CALLUM *jumps up and hugs* JUDE.

I've missed you.

JUDE. Get off. Are you mad or what?

He sits down with CALLUM.

Stop grinning like an idiot!

CALLUM. It's great to see you too! Where've you been? I really have missed you.

JUDE. I've been keeping my head down for a while.

CALLUM. You know about Dad?

JUDE. Of course. And now it's payback time.

CALLUM. What d'you mean?

Pause.

JUDE. I hear they booted you out of Heathcroft.

CALLUM. I wasn't booted. I walked.

JUDE. Good for you. That wasn't the place for you, little brother.

CALLUM. I know that now.

JUDE. It's a shame you didn't listen to me when I told you months ago. It would've saved you a lot of grief.

CALLUM *shrugs.*

So what're you up to these days?

CALLUM. Let's put it this way, hanging around in burger bars is the highlight.

JUDE. Would you like to do something more worthwhile?

CALLUM. Like what?

JUDE. I have to go now. Someone will be in touch.

CALLUM. Jude, don't do your man-of-mystery routine on me. What am I meant to tell Mum?

JUDE. Don't tell her anything. Where we're going, she can't follow.

CALLUM. And where are we going?

JUDE. I think you know, little brother.

CALLUM. Stop calling me that. What're you up to, Jude?

JUDE. Just tell me one thing. Are you in or out?

Pause.

Well?

Pause.

This is your chance to make a difference.

CALLUM. I'm in.

JUDE. Go home, pack your bags and make your peace with Mum. Report to this address at seven o'clock. You won't be seeing Mum – or anyone else for that matter – for a while.

CALLUM. No one at all?

JUDE. No. Are you still in?

  CALLUM *nods*.

  Welcome to the lifeboat party, little brother. I hope I can trust you.

Scene Sixteen

Callum's Bedroom at his Aunt's.

CALLUM *packs a suitcase on one side of the space and* SEPHY *does the same on the other. Enter* MEGGIE. *She's aged considerably.*

MEGGIE. What're you doing?

CALLUM. I'm going away.

MEGGIE. I see.

CALLUM. Tonight.

  Pause.

MEGGIE. When will you be back?

CALLUM. I don't know.

MEGGIE. I suppose you'll be seeing your brother.

CALLUM. I don't know. Probably.

MEGGIE. How is he?

  Pause.

  You know I don't want you to go.

CALLUM. Apart from you, I've got nothing to keep me here. And I need to do something for Dad.

MEGGIE. And he needed to do something for your sister. Where does it stop, Callum? When they've killed the lot of us?

CALLUM. It's up to them to stop it first.

MEGGIE. Do one thing for me.

CALLUM. What's that?

MEGGIE. Keep your head down. And tell your brother to do the same.

CALLUM. Okay, Mum.

They hug.

I'll go out the back.

He exits. The doorbell rings. MEGGIE *goes offstage to answer it.*

MEGGIE (*offstage*). Hello, Sarah.

SARAH (*offstage*). I have a letter for Callum. Is he in?

Scene Seventeen

Sephy's Bedroom. Rain outside.

SEPHY *finishes packing. She goes to the window.*

SEPHY (*to audience*). He's coming. He's not going to come. He's coming. He's not going to come. He's –

JASMINE (*offstage*). Persephone, move it. The car is waiting.

SEPHY. I'll be there in a moment!

She goes to the window.

Where is he?

MINERVA *enters.*

MINERVA. Enjoy yourself, Sephy.

SEPHY. Take care of Mum.

MINERVA *nods*.

Pause.

MINERVA. You lay off the booze, okay?

SEPHY. I'll try.

MINERVA. You better. I haven't got the energy to look after two of you.

JASMINE (*offstage*). Sephy, please, come on!

MINERVA. Bye then.

MINERVA *leans forward and awkwardly kisses* SEPHY *on the cheek.* MINERVA *exits.* SEPHY *looks through the window.*

JASMINE (*offstage*). Sephy!

She closes her case. She goes to look out of the window.

SEPHY. He's not coming.

She picks up her case and leaves.

Okay, Mother.

We hear the front door close, car door slam. The car starts up and drives off.

Scene Eighteen

Sephy's House.

SEPHY (*to audience*). Minerva was right. Chivers turned out to be a blessing in disguise. It gave me the chance to remake myself, from scratch. And I joined a dissident group. We were Crosses fighting for a change in the system. We moved quietly but irrevocably, like a relentless army of tiny termites eating away at the rotten fabric of a house. And we would succeed. We had to.

(*To audience*.) I admit that I thought about Callum. Often. But I've stopped yearning for the impossible. Maybe in a parallel universe, Callum and I could be together. But not here. Not now.

(*To audience*.) I'd finished my end-of-year exams and the summer holidays had already started. Over two-and-a-half years away from home and, to be honest, I had no desire whatsoever to return. But this time, Mother wasn't taking no for an answer. I'd run out of excuses. Arriving home was a real downer. The temptation to start drinking again was huge. Until Sarah whipped out a folded brown envelope from her pocket and stuffed it into my hand. I recognised the handwriting at once.

CALLUM *enters as she reads*.

CALLUM. . . . Dear Sephy, I know it's been a long time since we met and you probably don't remember me any more. But if you do, please could we meet tonight around nine o'clock at our special place. It's very important. But I'll understand if you can't make it. Two, almost three years is a long time. A lifetime. Callum.

SEPHY *ponders over whether she should go as we start to hear the sound of the waves*.

Scene Nineteen

The Beach. Night-time.

SEPHY *looks at her watch*. CALLUM *appears and sneaks up behind her*.

CALLUM. Surprise!

SEPHY. There you are. You gave me such a shock!

Silence.

What's wrong?

CALLUM suddenly kisses SEPHY. MORGAN, PETE and JUDE approach behind SEPHY. Their faces are masked. CALLUM stops kissing SEPHY.

CALLUM. I'm sorry.

She turns. She tries to escape.

JUDE. Over here, Pete.

PETE. Morgan!

She runs into the sea. The NOUGHTS follow with torches. They grab her. There is now a struggle in the water. Sometimes people are above the surface, sometimes below. They try to grab her and she breaks free. CALLUM joins in. After a while, JUDE grabs SEPHY. She hits JUDE.

JUDE. Bloody Dagger bitch.

JUDE punches SEPHY in the stomach.

That's for my sister.

She is winded. One of the other NOUGHTS grabs her, and they start dragging her out of the water. One of the NOUGHTS takes a hood out of his pocket. They cover her. She passes out.

Scene Twenty

The Hideaway.

CALLUM (*to audience*). We'd succeeded. We had Sephy. NO! Not Sephy . . . just a Cross – who deserved everything she got, who'd get us everything we needed. We bundled her into the boot of the car. And now we were in the middle of nowhere. Where no one would ever find her. Weren't we clever?

JUDE. I didn't think you had it in you, little brother.

CALLUM *grabs* JUDE.

CALLUM. Don't you ever doubt my loyalty again. D'you understand me?

MORGAN *steps forward and* PETE *stops him.*

D'you understand?

JUDE. So the mouse can roar, can he?

CALLUM *tightens his grip.*

Cool it, brother. Peace.

CALLUM *lets him go.*

PETE. What's our next move?

MORGAN. I dunno.

JUDE. We deliver the ransom note with proof we have her to the girl's father.

CALLUM. What proof?

JUDE. What would you suggest, little brother?

CALLUM. I'll cut off some of her hair. And film her holding today's paper.

PETE. Maybe we need something more convincing than her hair.

CALLUM. Something of hers that's bloodstained might be more effective.

JUDE. Good idea. What would you suggest?

MORGAN. Her ear!

CALLUM. Leave it to me. I'll sort it out.

Everyone stares at CALLUM.

What are you lot staring at?

The REPORTER *enters.*

REPORTER. The wife of Deputy Prime Minister Kamal Hadley was today admitted to the Haven Clinic, reportedly suffering from nervous exhaustion. The clinic, whose previous patients have included many celebrities, is renowned for treating people with alcohol and drug problems. In a statement issued this morning, Mr Hadley urged the media to be respectful of Mrs Hadley's privacy at this difficult time.

Scene Twenty-One

Sephy's Cell.

CALLUM *holds a camcorder.*

CALLUM (*to audience*). I paused outside the cell door. I could do this. I had to do this. It wasn't Sephy in there. She was just some Cross female who we needed to get us what we wanted.

CALLUM *removes her hood. Their eyes meet.* JUDE *stands behind* CALLUM.

I want you to hold this newspaper.

SEPHY. Why?

JUDE. We need to film you holding today's paper.

SEPHY *notices* JUDE *for the first time.*

SEPHY. Jude! Might have known you were behind this.

CALLUM. It wasn't just him.

SEPHY. Whatever. I'm not going to help you.

JUDE *holds* SEPHY *down.*

JUDE. Hold that paper or we'll break your arms.

CALLUM (*to* JUDE). I don't need you standing over me, supervising.

JUDE. Not supervising. Just observing.

CALLUM. Hold the newspaper, Sephy.

CALLUM *holds the newspaper out.* SEPHY *takes it.* LEILA, *a fellow Nought kidnapper, enters.*

LEILA. I've come to see the daughter of the famous Kamal Hadley.

CALLUM. I don't need an audience, thanks.

LEILA. Let's see the silver spoon then.

CALLUM. Leila!

LEILA. I bet you've never had more to worry about in life than chipping the odd fingernail.

JUDE. Leila, go and guard the front. Morgan, you go with her.

LEILA (*to* CALLUM). Later, sweetie.

LEILA *kisses* CALLUM *and leaves with* MORGAN.

SEPHY. Is that your girlfriend?

CALLUM *hands* SEPHY *a sheet of paper.*

CALLUM. I want you to read out that message for your father.

CALLUM *points the camcorder at her.*

SEPHY (*to camera*). Dad, don't give them a penny.

SEPHY *scrunches the paper up and throws it away.* JUDE *rushes over and grabs her.*

JUDE. You're not in control in here. We are. And you will do as you're told or you won't leave this place alive. Do you understand?

JUDE *drops her.*

You won't get away with your crap around here. We're not your servants any more.

CALLUM. I'll handle this.

JUDE *goes to exit. He turns back.*

JUDE. Make sure she does as she's told.

JUDE *goes out.* CALLUM *picks up paper and starts smoothing it out.*

SEPHY. I understand why you feel you have to do something. I really do. But this isn't the way.

Pause.

Callum, listen to me. At Chivers I became involved in protests and debates and sit-ins . . . If you try to change the world using violence, you'll just swap one form of injustice for –

CALLUM. I don't want your ruddy advice, thank you. I'm sick of your charity and your handouts. You're just like all the others. You think we Noughts can't do a damned thing unless you Crosses are there to help or supervise.

SEPHY. Don't hate me for wanting to make a difference. I genuinely –

CALLUM. Shut up! Hold up the newspaper and read the words on this.

CALLUM *hands her the newspaper and holds up the sheet.*

Read it.

SEPHY. Callum, please.

CALLUM. READ IT.

She reads from the paper. CALLUM *films her.*

SEPHY. 'Dad, I've been kidnapped and the kidnappers say you'll never see me again unless you do exactly as you're told. Your instructions will be in the envelope along with this tape. You have twenty-four hours to follow their demands to the letter. If you don't, I'll be killed.'

SEPHY *is crying.* CALLUM *zooms in. She wipes her eyes. He finishes filming. He takes out a pair of scissors.*

CALLUM. Now, take your top off.

SEPHY. Pardon?

CALLUM. You heard me.

SEPHY. No way.

CALLUM. Take off your top or I'll do it for you.

She starts taking her top off. He turns away.

SEPHY. Are you going to kill me, Callum?

CALLUM. Just be quiet.

SEPHY. Didn't that night mean anything to you?

Pause.

It wasn't me who killed your father, Callum. I wanted him to live as much as you did.

CALLUM. You and your kind killed him.

SEPHY. So now you're going to kill me. But not you personally, I bet. That's not your style, is it?

CALLUM. You wouldn't be the first Dagger I've killed. Not by a long shot.

SEPHY. And I'd be easy to kill, wouldn't I? 'Cause I don't count. I'm nothing. A black Dagger bitch. Just like you're a white Blanker bastard.

CALLUM grabs SEPHY and cuts her finger. He wipes the blood on her top.

CALLUM. That'll prove we mean business.

SEPHY. Now your brother really will be impressed.

SEPHY puts her finger in her mouth. CALLUM takes his jacket off and puts it on her shoulders. She shrugs it off.

CALLUM. Suit yourself.

CALLUM goes to leave.

SEPHY. When you all decide you don't need me any more, I want *you* to do it.

CALLUM exits.

Scene Twenty-Two

The Hideaway.

CALLUM (*to audience*). We sent off the tape with Sephy's top.
  And the next day we all gathered round the TV for the
  evening news.

  JUDE *flicks on the TV.* CALLUM, JUDE, LEILA, PETE *and*
  MORGAN *watch the TV. Enter* KAMAL *and* REPORTERS.

KAMAL. I am here to announce that I shall be temporarily with-
  drawing from public office for personal family reasons. I don't
  wish to say anything further at this time.

  JUDE *flicks off the TV.* KAMAL *exits.*

MORGAN. Bastard.

JUDE. We've got him over a barrel.

PETE. I don't trust him.

JUDE. I don't trust any of them.

PETE. What's the plan for the telephone relay?

JUDE. Leila should stay here with the girl.

LEILA. My pleasure.

JUDE. Pete, Morgan and I will make our relay phone calls from
  three different locations around town to stop them tracing the
  calls. Callum will drop off the second set of instructions, pick
  up our money and head straight back here.

PETE. I think it's better if Leila makes the pick-up. That's always
  the most dangerous part and, as a girl, she's more likely to go
  unnoticed.

CALLUM. Then I'll go in your place and make one of the
  phone calls.

LEILA. Make your mind up, guys.

JUDE. No. Of all of us, you're the one Hadley knows the best.
  We can't take any chances of him recognising your voice.

PETE. Good thinking.

CALLUM. I'm not staying here. I'm not a ruddy babysitter.

JUDE. You don't have a choice.

CALLUM. I'm not staying here.

JUDE. You're staying behind and that's final. Let's go. And remember, Sephy Hadley won't see her dad again till five LM members are released.

They all get ready to leave.

If the police or anyone suspicious arrives, you shoot the girl first and ask questions afterwards. Get it?

CALLUM. Got it.

PETE. Good.

JUDE. We're counting on you.

LEILA *kisses* CALLUM.

LEILA. Give her a kick from me.

They leave CALLUM *on his own.*

Scene Twenty-Three

Sephy's Cell.

CALLUM *approaches* SEPHY *with a bowl of soup.*

SEPHY (*to audience*). Even if he'd forced me, I couldn't have looked at Callum. I'd never give him the satisfaction. To look at him would be to weep and scream and beg. And I wasn't going to do any of those things. Ever. He was one of them now.

SEPHY *is lying down and rubbing her stomach.*

CALLUM *sits down on her mattress and puts the bowl down.* CALLUM *moves her hand away and rubs her stomach.*

What are you doing?

CALLUM. You're in pain.

SEPHY. Like you care.

CALLUM. Of course I care.

SEPHY. Then let me go. Please.

CALLUM. I can't.

Pause.

I love you.

SEPHY. Then let me go.

CALLUM. I wanted to tell you once before. I was afraid to say it. But I'm not any more.

SEPHY. Love doesn't exist between a Nought and a Cross. You told me before.

CALLUM. I thought we were going to go away together. I guess you went off the idea.

SEPHY. Didn't you get my letter?

CALLUM. What letter?

SEPHY *is crying.*

SEPHY. Ignore me. Just go away, please.

CALLUM. Do you hate me?

Pause.

Do you?

SEPHY (*to audience*). Before I could make a sound, his lips were on mine and I could see nothing but his face, his eyes.

CALLUM (*to audience*). I'd daydreamed so many times of doing this. This was something that was never, ever going to happen.

SEPHY (*to audience*). But now the world had turned upside-down and Callum was kissing me.

CALLUM (*to audience*). This wasn't real. None of it was real. It couldn't be. It was forbidden. Against the law. Against nature.

SEPHY (*to audience*). I was dreaming again. Lost in my world where there were no Noughts and Crosses. Just me and Callum, as Callum and I should be.

CALLUM (*to audience*). Perhaps if we could just love long enough and hard enough and deep enough, then the world outside would never, ever hurt us again.

SEPHY. Callum!

CALLUM. Shh! I won't hurt you. I'd never hurt you.

SEPHY (*to audience*). His breath was hot and made my insides melt.

CALLUM. I love you.

SEPHY (*to audience*). I pulled him closer to me, wrapping my arms around him.

BOTH (*to audience*). And then, it was as if we'd both caught fire.

CALLUM (*to audience*). Sort of like spontaneous combustion,

SEPHY (*to audience*). and we were burning up.

CALLUM. I love you.

SEPHY (*to audience*). I could hardly hear him over the blood roaring in my ears. Every caress, every stroke robbed me of my breath and burnt through my skin.

CALLUM (*to audience*). She unbuttoned my shirt.

SEPHY (*to audience*). He unfastened my bra.

CALLUM (*to audience*). She unzipped my trousers.

BOTH (*to audience*). We were both naked.

CALLUM (*to audience*). And I was shaking. But not from the cold.

BOTH (*to audience*). We both knelt on the bed facing each other.

SEPHY (*to audience*). Callum's gaze moved down over my body.

CALLUM (*to audience*). I reached out and touched her face.

SEPHY (*to audience*). He ran his hands over my lips and my nose and forehead.

CALLUM (*to audience*). I lay her down gently.

SEPHY (*to audience*). His hands and lips exploring my body.

BOTH (*to audience*). We were going to make this time last for ever.

SEPHY (*to audience*). I let myself drift away, following wherever Callum led. Beside him all the way as he led me across the frontier into a new real, unreal world.

BOTH (*to audience*). Not quite heaven. Not quite hell.

CALLUM *and* SEPHY *sit on the mattress.* SEPHY *is crying.* CALLUM *tries to put his arm around her. She pulls away and puts on her sweater.* JUDE *and* MORGAN *enter.*

CALLUM. What's happened?

JUDE. You tell us.

CALLUM. Where's Leila?

MORGAN. Arrested.

CALLUM. What? Where's Pete?

JUDE. Dead.

CALLUM. What?

JUDE. They had undercover police everywhere. They must have been monitoring every phone box in town. We were lucky to escape in one piece. I'd thought we could take the girl and move out of here to somewhere safer . . .

CALLUM. I'll pack up our equipment.

JUDE. I don't think so. Morgan, go and pack up everything essential. Leave the rest.

MORGAN *goes out.* JUDE *switches the light on.* SEPHY *weeps.*

You stupid, stupid berk. We're finished.

JUDE *grabs* CALLUM. *He hits* CALLUM *as he speaks:*

We could have got what we wanted and let her go. They'd never have found us. But not now. Why d'you have to rape her? You stupid, stupid . . .

CALLUM *punches* JUDE *in the face and* JUDE *falls to the ground.*

CALLUM. Don't you ever hit me again as long as you live.

JUDE *gets up and attacks* CALLUM. *They fight. While they fight,* SEPHY *rushes to the door.*

JUDE. Stop her! Get her! Morgan!

SEPHY *has gone. They follow her.*

Scene Twenty-Four

The Forest.

SEPHY *weaves around the trees.* CALLUM, JUDE *and* MORGAN *follow with torches.* SEPHY *hides behind a tree.*

MORGAN. Over there!

JUDE. Persephone!

Pause.

I know you can hear me. We're kilometres away from anywhere here. It's no good trying to run.

Pause.

You'll wander around this forest for days without seeing another soul. There's no food. No water. Come out now and we won't harm you. We promise.

Pause.

If you don't show yourself and we find you . . .

JUDE *signals to the others and they separate off.*

(*Wandering off.*) Sephy, I know you're here somewhere.

SEPHY *is close to* CALLUM. *She appears from behind a tree.* CALLUM *spots her. He approaches her from behind and grabs her. He puts his hand over her mouth.*

CALLUM. Shh. It's me.

MORGAN (*calling*). What was that?

CALLUM. It's only me. I tripped.

MORGAN. I'll go towards the road.

CALLUM. What's that over there? I think it's her. She must be trying to double back on us. Heading for the cabin.

JUDE. Where? Morgan, over here.

MORGAN *and* JUDE *head off.* SEPHY *and* CALLUM *are alone.*

CALLUM. Do you see Orion's Belt?

SEPHY *nods.*

Always keep it immediately behind you. When you reach the road, turn left onto it and keep going.

SEPHY. Callum . . .

CALLUM. Quickly, Sephy.

SEPHY. It's not too late for us to escape.

CALLUM. I'll come and find you, Sephy.

They kiss.

Now go.

SEPHY *leaves.*

Scene Twenty-Five

Outside a Private Hospital.

KAMAL *enters with* JUNO, *surrounded by* REPORTERS. *He holds a sheet of paper.*

KAMAL. I . . . I will make a short statement and . . . that's it. (*Reading from the sheet.*) 'My daughter is still unconscious after being found this morning. Her doctors describe her condition as critical but stable. The police are present and will interview her as soon as she regains consciousness. Acting on information received, we captured one of the kidnappers and another opened fire on the police and was killed as a result. No ransom was paid.' That's all I'd like to say at this moment.

He goes to exit, trailed by JOURNALISTS *including the* REPORTER.

REPORTER. How many kidnappers were there?

JOURNALIST 1. Where was your daughter held during her ordeal?

JOURNALIST 2. What are the extent of her injuries?

Scene Twenty-Six

Sephy's House. The kitchen.

SEPHY (*to audience*). Four weeks later, after my fifth morning of waking up feeling like last Crossmas's leftover turkey, I found myself in the kitchen making some dry toast and weak blackcurrant tea.

MINERVA. Oh, there you are. You okay?

SEPHY. Yes. Apart from this tummy bug.

MINERVA. You've been sick for the last couple of mornings, haven't you?

SEPHY. How do you know?

MINERVA. I've heard you calling on the porcelain telephone!

Pause.

When're you going to talk about what happened to you when you were kidnapped?

SEPHY. Never.

MINERVA. You shouldn't bottle it up inside.

SEPHY. Back off, Minerva, okay? My being kidnapped won't reflect badly on you in any way, shape or form, so you can leave me alone.

MINERVA. What are you talking about? I'm concerned about you.

SEPHY. Yeah, right!

MINERVA. What happened to you out there?

SEPHY. I was kidnapped. I escaped. Now you know as much as I do.

MINERVA. Did anyone . . . hurt you?

SEPHY. Not really.

MINERVA. You can tell me. I won't mention it to Dad, or to Mum when she gets out of rehab. I promise.

Pause.

And they'll catch the kidnappers any day now. I overheard Dad talking about it. So you won't be protecting anyone by keeping quiet.

SEPHY. I don't want to talk about it.

MINERVA. Sephy, are . . . are you pregnant?

SEPHY. What're you talking about? Of course I'm . . . not . . .

MINERVA. So you could be?

Pause.

Who was it, Sephy? Who attacked you? You can tell me. I won't tell anyone, I promise.

SEPHY. Just because I've been a bit sick in the mornings . . . That doesn't mean anything. It's just a delayed reaction to everything that's happened to me over the last few weeks. Okay?

MINERVA. Okay.

MINERVA *exits*. SEPHY *is horrified*.

Scene Twenty-Seven

The Prison.

CALLUM *is sitting on the floor with his Cross prison guard,* JACK. *They play cards.*

CALLUM. Your mind isn't on this game, is it?

JACK. I don't want to play any more.

CALLUM. I thought I was supposed to be the moody one.

Pause.

What time is it, Jack?

JACK. Ten to.

CALLUM. Time for a quick game of rummy.

JACK. Callum . . .

CALLUM *puts down the cards.*

Pause.

CALLUM. Do you ever wonder what it would be like if our positions were reversed? If we whites were in charge instead of you Crosses?

JACK. Can't say I'd ever thought about it.

CALLUM. I used to think about it a lot. A world with no more discrimination or prejudice. A level playing field.

JACK. Is that a theory or a fairy tale?

CALLUM. It's just something I used to think about.

JACK. We'll always find a way to mess up, doesn't matter who's in charge. It's human nature.

CALLUM. You think so?

JACK *shrugs*.

You don't believe that things get better? That they have to one day, some day?

JACK. When?

CALLUM. It takes a long time.

JACK. But they do?

CALLUM. They do.

JACK. I hope so. Your girl, Persephone Hadley, tried to get in here to see you – and more than once as well. But orders came from way above the Governor's head that you were to have no visitors whatsoever, under any circumstances.

Pause.

CALLUM. Jack, can I ask you a favour?

JACK. Just name it.

CALLUM. It might get you into trouble.

JACK. My dull life could do with a bit of sprucing up.

CALLUM. Could you find a way to deliver this letter to Sephy?

CALLUM *takes an envelope out of his pocket.*

JACK. Persephone Hadley?

CALLUM. That's right.

JACK. Sure thing.

CALLUM *gives* JACK *the envelope.*

CALLUM. You have to personally put it in her hand. Promise?

JACK. I promise.

> *There is the sound of a key in the cell door.* JACK *hides the letter. In walks* KAMAL *and the* PRISON GOVERNOR.

KAMAL. You can leave us now, Governor.

GOVERNOR. We'll wait outside, Officer.

> JACK *and the* GOVERNOR *exit.*

KAMAL. I'm sure you can guess why I'm here.

> CALLUM *doesn't answer.*

> I'm here to offer you a deal. It's not too late for me to overturn the sentence. If you do what I say, I'll make sure you don't hang. You'll be sentenced to life and I'll make sure you only serve eight to ten years. You'll come out of prison with your whole life ahead of you.

CALLUM. And what exactly do I have to do for this . . . largesse?

KAMAL. Sign this.

CALLUM. What does it say?

KAMAL. It states that you raped my daughter and you want nothing to do with her unborn child.

CALLUM. Sephy knows that's not true.

KAMAL. If you tell her you don't want to be a father to the child, she'll terminate the pregnancy. Then we can all get on with our lives.

CALLUM. Is it just the thought of Sephy and I having a child together that you can't stand, or is it mixed-race children in general?

> *The door opens. The* GOVERNOR *and* JACK *enter.*

GOVERNOR. I need to open the public gallery, sir.

KAMAL. Are you going to save your life or the child's?

> CALLUM *tears up the confession.*

> (*As he leaves the cell.*) Have it your way.

GOVERNOR. Do you have any last requests?

CALLUM. Just get it over with.

GOVERNOR. Do you want a priest?

CALLUM shakes his head. GOVERNOR *nods at* JACK *and exits.*

JACK. Put your hands behind your back, Callum.

JACK handcuffs CALLUM.

Not long now.

They walk down a corridor. Nought PRISONERS *reach out to* CALLUM.

PRISONER 1. Good luck, Cal.

PRISONER 2. Spit in their eye, Callum.

PRISONER 3. Good luck.

JACK. Please forgive me, Callum –

CALLUM. You've got a job to do. It's not your fault.

JACK shakes CALLUM's *hand.*

The execution chamber, with a noose and a platform. A large CROWD *of spectators enter.* MINERVA *has her arm around* SEPHY. KAMAL *and* JASMINE *are also there.* JACK *puts the hood over* CALLUM's *head. Blackout. The prison clock chimes one.*

SEPHY. I love you, Callum.

Two.

I love you and our child will love you too.

Three.

I love you, Callum, I'll always love you.

Four.

CALLUM. I love you too, Sephy.

Five.

SEPHY. I love you, Callum.

Six.

CALLUM. I love –

We hear the trapdoor give way and the sound of CALLUM*'s body swinging. Out of the darkness, we hear the* REPORTER.

REPORTER. And last night at midnight, Deputy Prime Minister Kemal Hadley's daughter, Persephone, gave birth to a girl. Miss Hadley has issued a statement that her daughter, named Callie Rose, will be taking her father's name of McGregor. The Deputy Prime Minister was unavailable for comment.

The lights come up on SEPHY *holding Callie Rose.* SEPHY *comforts her daughter.*

Lights fade.

The End.